KB054191

직독직해로 읽는

플란다스의 개
A Dog of Flanders

직독직해로 읽는

플란다스의 개

A Dog of Flanders

개정판 2쇄 발행 2020년 12월 20일
초판 1쇄 발행 2010년 12월 30일

원작	위다
역주	더 콜링(김정희, 박윤수, 이성진, 이은신)
디자인	DX
일러스트	정은수
발행인	조경아
발행처	랭귀지북스
주소	서울시 마포구 포은로2나길 31 벨라비스타 208호
전화	02.406.0047 **팩스** 02.406.0042
이메일	languagebooks@hanmail.net
MP3 다운로드	blog.naver.com/languagebook
등록번호	101-90-85278 **등록일자** 2008년 7월 10일
ISBN	979-11-5635-044-6 (13740)
가격	12,000원

ⓒ LanguageBooks 2010

이 도서의 국립중앙도서관 출판예정도서목록(CIP)은 서지정보유통지원시스템 홈페이지(http://seoji.nl.go.kr)와
국가자료공동목록시스템(http://www.nl.go.kr/kolisnet)에서 이용하실 수 있습니다. (CIP제어번호 : CIP2016006150)

직독직해로 읽는

플란다스의 개
A Dog of Flanders

위다 원작
더 콜링 역주

Language Books

머리말

"어렸을 때 누구나 갖고 있던 세계명작 한 질.
그리고 TV에서 하던 세계명작 만화에 대한 추억이 있습니다."

"친숙한 이야기를 영어 원문으로 읽어 봐야겠다고 마음먹고 샀던 원서들은
이제 애물단지가 되어 버렸습니다."

"재미있는 세계명작 하나 읽어 보려고 따져 보는 어려운 영문법.
모르는 단어 찾느라 이리저리 뒤져 봐야 하는 사전.
몇 장 넘겨 보기도 전에 지칩니다."

　영어 독해력을 기르려면 술술 읽어가며 내용을 파악하는 것
이 중요합니다. 현재 수능 시험에도 대세인 '직독직해' 스타일을
접목시킨 〈직독직해로 읽는 세계명작 시리즈〉는 세계명작을 영어
원작으로 쉽게 읽어갈 수 있도록 안내해 드릴 것입니다.

　'직독직해' 스타일로 읽다 보면, 영문법을 들먹이며 따질 필요
가 없으니 쉽고, 끊어 읽다 보니 독해 속도도 빨라집니다. 이 습관
이 들여지면 어떤 글을 만나도 두렵지 않을 것입니다.

　명작의 재미를 즐기며 영어 독해력을 키우는 두 마리의 토
끼를 잡으세요!

〈직독직해로 읽는 세계명작 시리즈〉 영원한 파트너 윤수와 번역하느라 고생한 성진, 은신 씨, 늦은 밤에도 꼼꼼하게 챙겨 주시던 디자인 DX, 무리한 스케줄에도 늘 가장 먼저 그림 완성해 주시던 일러스트레이터 은수 씨, 그리고 이 책이 출판될 수 있도록 언제나 든든하게 지원해 주시는 랭귀지북스에 감사의 마음을 전합니다.

마지막으로 내 삶의 유일한 소망되시는 하나님께 영광을 올려 드립니다.

더 콜링 김정희

목차

C O N T E N T S

Nello and Patrasche were left / all alone / in the world.
넬로와 파트라슈는 남겨졌다   외톨이로   세상에

They were friends / in a friendship / closer than
그들은 친구였다   우정을 나눈   형제보다 더 가까운.

brotherhood. Nello was a little *Ardennois / —— Patrasche
넬로는 아르덴 출신의 소년이었고   — 파트라슈는 커다란

was a big **Fleming. They were both of the same age / by
플란다스 개였다.   둘 다 같은 나이였다

length of years, / yet / one was still young, / and the other
햇수로 치자면,   하지만   하나는 아직 어렸고,

was already old. They had dwelt together / almost all their
다른 하나는 이미 늙었다.   그들은 같이 살았었다   인생의 거의 전부를:

days: / both were orphaned and destitute, / and owed their
둘 다 고아가 되었고 가난했으며,

lives to the same hand. It had been the beginning / of the
같은 사람에게 의지하여 살았었다.   그것이 시작이었다

tie between them, / their first bond of sympathy; / and it
둘 사이를 이어 준,   연민이라는 첫 번째 유대가;

had strengthened / day by day, / and had grown / with their
그리고 그 유대는 튼튼해지고   나날이,   커져으며   그들이 성장함에

growth, / firm and indissoluble, / until they loved / one
따라,   단단하고 떼어놓을 수 없게 되어,   마침내 그들은 사랑하게 되었다

another / very greatly. Their home was a little hut / on the
서로를   매우.   그들의 집은 작은 오두막이었다

edge of a little village / —— a Flemish village / a ***league
작은 마을 변두리에 있는   — 플란다스 지역의 마을인

from ****Antwerp, / set amidst flat breadths of pasture
안트베르펜에서 조금 떨어진,   넓게 펼쳐진 목초지와 밭 한 가운데 있는,

and corn-lands, / with long lines of poplars and of alders
길게 늘어선 포플러 나무와 오리 나무가

/ bending in the breeze / on the edge of the great canal /
바람에 흔들거리는   커다란 운하 가장자리에 있는

* 아르덴 사람(아르덴(Ardennes)은 프랑스 북동부 지역과 접한 벨기에의 고산 지대)
** 플랑드르 지방의 사람(플랑드르(Flandre)은 벨기에 서부를 중심으로 네덜란드 서부와 프랑스 북부에 걸친
지역으로 영어로는 플란다스(Flanders)라고 한다)
*** 거리의 단위로써 1리그는 약 5Km 거리
**** 플란다스 지역에 위치한 벨기에의 항구 도시

which ran through it. It had about a score of houses and
마을을 가로지르는.   그 마을에는 약 20채의 집과 농가들이 있었다,

homesteads, / with shutters of bright green or sky-blue, /
                                하늘색 덧문을 가졌고,

and roofs rose-red or black and white, / and walls white-
장밋빛 혹은 검은색과 흰색이 섞인 지붕과,   흰색으로 칠한 벽을 가진

washed / until they shone in the sun like snow. In the centre
               햇빛을 받아 눈처럼 빛나는.

of the village / stood a windmill, / placed on a little moss-
마을 한가운데에는   풍차가 서 있었다,   이끼가 살짝 낀 비탈진 곳에:

grown slope: / it was a landmark / to all the level country
                    그것은 이정표였다   비슷한 높이에 있는 지역들을 위한.

round.

Key Expression

문장부호 대시, 세미콜론, 콜론의 쓰임

첫 페이지부터 대시(——)나 세미콜론(;)과 같은 문장부호가 자주 등장하는데요. 이들 문장부호의 쓰임을 알아볼까요.

▶ —— (대시)

보충 설명에 쓰이는 문장부호입니다. '즉, ~'이나 '그리고~'라고 해석하면 됩니다. 여기는 대시와 닫는 대시가 함께 쓰이는데, 뒤에 쉼표나 마침표가 올 때에는 대시가 하나만 쓰입니다.

ex) Nello was a little Ardennois —— Patrasche was a big Fleming.

넬로는 아르덴 출신의 소년이었고, —— 파트라슈는 커다란 플란다스의 개였다.

▶ ; (세미콜론)

','(쉼표)+접속사'의 축약형으로 and, but, or, for 등을 대신하여 쓰입니다. 문장에 따라 '그리고(그래서), 그러나(반면에), 왜냐하면' 등으로 해석합니다.

ex) For Patrasche was their alpha and omega; their treasury and granary; their store of gold and wand of wealth; …

파트라슈는 그들의 모두였기 때문에; 그리고 그들의 금고이자 창고였고, 보물 창고이자 마법의 지팡이였으며; …

▶ : (콜론)

콜론은 무언가를 열거할 때 사용하며, '말하자면(동격), 예를 들면(예시), ~라고(인용)' 등의 의미로도 쓰입니다.

ex) They had dwelt together almost all their days: both were orphaned and destitute, and owed their lives to the same hand.

그들은 거의 인생 전부를 함께 했다: 말하자면 둘 다 고아였고 가난했으며 같은 사람에게 의지했다.

---

brotherhood 형제애 | almost all 거의 전부 | orphan (아이를) 고아로 만들다 | destitute 가난한 | sympathy 연민
| strengthen 튼튼하게 하다, 강화하다 | day by day 날이날 | indissoluble 서로 떼어놓을 수 없는 | hut 오두막 |
edge 변두리 | amidst (amid의 동의어) 가운데 | breadth 넓게 펼쳐진, 너비 | pasture 목초지 | poplar 포플러 나무 |
alder 오리 나무 | canal 운하 | score 20개 | homestead 농가 | shutter 덧문 | moss 이끼 | landmark 이정표

9

It had once been painted scarlet, / sails and all, / but that had
풍차는 한때 주홍색으로 칠해졌었다   날개와 모든 것이,   하지만 그때는 풍차

been in its infancy, / half a century or more earlier, / when it
가 처음 지어졌을 때였다,   반세기 전쯤 또는 그 이전,

had ground wheat / for the soldiers of Napoleon; / and it was
밀을 빻던 시절에   나폴레옹의 군사들을 위해서;   그리고 이제는

now a ruddy brown, / tanned by wind and weather. It went
불그스름한 갈색이 되었다,   바람과 날씨에 시달리면서.   풍차는 괴상하

queerly / by fits and starts, / as though rheumatic and stiff in
게 움직였다   멈췄다 움직였다 하면서   마치 류머티즘에 걸려 뻣뻣해진 관절처럼

the joints / from age, / but it served the whole neighborhood,
나이가 들어서,   그래도 모든 마을 사람들에게 도움을 주었다,

/ which would have thought it almost as impious / to carry
그리고 사람들은 거의 불경스러운 일이라고 생각했다   곡식을 다른

grain elsewhere / as to attend / any other religious service
곳으로 가져가는 것은   마치 참여하는 것처럼   다른 종교 행사에

/ than the mass / that was performed / at the altar / of the
미사가 아닌   열리는   제단에서

little old gray church, / with its conical steeple, / which
작고 오래된 회색 교회의,   원뿔 모양을 한 교회의 첨탑을 가진,

stood opposite to it, / and whose single bell rang / morning,
교회는 풍차 건너편에 서 있었고,   교회의 단 하나의 종은 울렸다   아침,

noon, and night / with that strange, subdued, hollow sadness
점심, 그리고 저녁에   이상하고, 나직하면서, 공허한 슬픔이 묻어나는 소리를

/ which every bell / that hangs in *the Low Countries /
모든 종들은   낮은 지대에 있는

seems to gain / as an integral part of its melody.
울리는 듯 하다   그런 멜로디로.

---

* 주로 벨기에와 네덜란드의 낮은 해안 지대를 뜻함

infancy 초창기 | grind 빻다 | ruddy 불그스름한 | impious 불경한 | altar 제단 | conical 원뿔의 | steeple 첨탑 |
subdue 가라앉히다 | integral part 전체의 일부 | spire 뾰족탑 | tideless 조수 간만의 차가 없는 | trample 짓밟다 |
tread 디디다, 밟아서 뭉개다 | furrow 고랑 | contrive 겨우 ~하다

Within sound of the little melancholy clock / almost from
그 작고 구슬픈 시계의 종소리가 들리는 곳에서

their birth upward, / they had dwelt together, / Nello and
태어나서 지금까지 대부분,   그들은 같이 살았다,   넬로와 파트라슈는,

Patrasche, / in the little hut on the edge of the village, /
마을 변두리의 작은 오두막에서,

with the cathedral spire of Antwerp / rising in the north-
안트베르펜 성당의 뾰족탑이   북동쪽으로 솟아 있는,

east, / beyond the great green plain / of seeding grass and
넓은 푸른 들판 너머로   풀과 옥수수를 파종하는

spreading corn / that stretched away from them / like a
멀리 펼쳐져 있는

tideless, changeless sea. It was the hut of a very old man,
파도가 없는, 잔잔한 바다처럼.   그곳은 나이 든 노인의 오두막이었다,

/ of a very poor man / —— of old Jehan Daas, / who in his
아주 가난한 사람인   — 늙은 예한 다스 할아버지의,

time had been a soldier, / and who remembered the wars
그는 젊었을 때에는 군인이었고,   전쟁을 기억하고 있었다

/ that had trampled the country / as oxen tread down the
그 땅을 짓밟았던   황소가 밭고랑을 밟아서 뭉개듯이,

furrows, / and who had brought from his service nothing /
그리고 그는 군대에서 빈손으로 돌아왔다

except a wound, / which had made him a cripple.
상처만 입은 채,   그를 절름발이로 만든.

When old Jehan Daas had reached his full eighty, / his
예한 다스 할아버지가 여든 살이 되었을 때,

daughter had died / in the Ardennes, / hard by Stavelot, /
그의 딸이 죽었고   아르덴 지역에 살던,   스타벨로트에서 매우 가까운,

and had left him / in legacy / her two-year-old son. The old
그에게 남겼다   유산으로   두 살 난 아들을.   할아버지는

man / could ill contrive to support himself, / but he took
겨우 자기 한 몸 먹고 살 정도였지만,   받아들였다

up / the additional burden / uncomplainingly, / and it soon
그 짐을   묵묵히,   그리고 그 짐은 머지

became / welcome and precious / to him. Little Nello / ——
않아 되었다   반갑고 소중한 존재가   할아버지에게. 어린 넬로는

which was but a pet diminutive **for Nicolas** —— / throve
— 니콜라스의 애칭인 —   할아버지와

with him, / and the old man and the little child / lived in
함께 잘 자랐다.   그리고 할아버지와 어린 아이는   가난한 작은

the poor little hut / contentedly.
오두막에서 살았다   만족하면서.

It was a very humble **little** mud-hut / indeed, / **but it was**
그 집은 매우 허름한 작은 흙집이었다   정말로,   하지만 그 집은

clean / and white as a sea-shell, / and stood / in a small
깨끗했고   조가비처럼 하얀 집으로,   서 있었다

plot of garden-ground / **that** yielded **beans and** herbs **and**
작은 텃밭에   콩과 허브와 호박들을 심은.

pumpkins. They were very poor, / terribly poor / ——
            그들은 매우 가난했다,   엄청 가난했다

many a day / they had nothing at all to eat. They never
— 며칠씩이나   먹을 것이 전혀 없었다.

by any chance **had enough: / to have had enough to eat /**
그들은 결코 우연이라도 풍족했던 적이 없다: 먹을 것이라도 충분히 있었더라면

would have been / to have reached paradise / at once.
여겼을 것이다   천국에 도착한 것이라고   당장.

But the old man was / very gentle and good to the boy, /
하지만 할아버지는   매우 상냥했고 소년에게 잘해 주었다,

and the boy was / a beautiful, innocent, **truthful,** tender-
그리고 소년은   아름답고, 순진하고, 정직하고, 마음씨 고운 아이였다;

hearted **creature; / and they were happy / on a crust and**
            그래서 그들은 행복했고

a few leaves of cabbage, / and asked no more / of earth or
빵 부스러기와 양배추 몇 잎으로도,   더 이상 바라지 않았다   땅의 것이나 하늘

heaven; / save indeed that / Patrasche should be always
의 것을;   정말 그것 말고는   파트라슈가 그들 곁에 있어 주는 것,

with them, / since without Patrasche / where would they
            파트라슈가 없다면   그들이 있을 곳은 어디였을까?

have been?

For Patrasche was their alpha and omega; / their treasury
왜냐하면 파트라슈가 그들의 전부였기 때문이었다;　　　　　　그들의 금고이자 창고였고;

and granary; / their store of gold and wand of wealth; /
금덩어리를 넣는 금고이자 부자를 만들어 주는 마법 지팡이였고;

their bread-winner and minister; / their only friend and
그들의 생계를 책임진 가장이자 일꾼이었으며;　　　　그들의 유일한 친구이자 위안을 주는

comforter. Patrasche dead or gone from them, / they must
존재였다.　　파트라슈가 죽거나 그들을 떠난다면,

have laid themselves down / and died likewise. Patrasche
그들 자신도 몸져 누워서　　　　　같은 식으로 죽었을 것이다.　　파트라슈는

was / body, brains, hands, head, and feet / to both of them:
몸, 지능, 손, 머리, 그리고 발이었다　　　　　　　그 둘에게 있어서:

/ Patrasche was their very life, / their very soul. For Jehan
파트라슈는 그들의 인생이었고,　　　　　그들의 영혼이었다.

Daas was old and a cripple, / and Nello was but a child; /
예한 다스는 늙고 불구였으며　　　　넬로는 아직 어린 아이였기 때문이다;

and Patrasche was their dog.
그리고 파트라슈는 그들의 그런 개였다.

A dog of Flanders / —— yellow of hide, / large of head and
플란다스의 개는　　　　　— 노란 털과,　　　　　큼직한 머리와 네 다리,

limb, / with wolf-like ears / that stood erect, / and legs
늑대 같은 귀를 지녔으며　　　번쩍 선,　　　　　그리고 다리는 활처럼

bowed / and feet widened / in the muscular development
구부러졌고　　발은 넓적했다　　　　근육이 발달해서

/ wrought in his breed / by many generations of hard
양육 과정에서 받은 괴롭힘에 의해　　대대로 힘든 일을 해 오면서.

service.

Patrasche came of a race / which had toiled hard and
파트라슈는 종족으로부터 태어났다　　힘들게 일했고 학대 받았으며

cruelly / from sire to son / in Flanders / many a century
대대로　　　플란다스에서　　수백 년 동안

/ —— slaves of slaves, / dogs of the people, / beasts of the
— 노예들의 노예였고,　　　하층민들의 개였으며,

shafts and the harness, / creatures that lived straining their
자루와 마구를 끄는 짐승이었고,　　죽도록 일하며 살다가

sinews / in the gall of the cart, / and died breaking their
수레에 피부가 쓸려서 벗겨지며,　　　그러다가 애끓으며 죽었다

hearts / on the flints of the streets.
길거리의 돌바닥에서.

Patrasche had been born / of parents who had labored
파트라슈는 태어났다   고된 일만 했던 부모에게서

hard / all their days / over the sharp-set stones / of the
평생 동안   날카로운 돌이 깔린 길 위에서

various cities / and the long, shadowless, weary roads /
여러 도시의   그리고 길고, 그늘도 없는, 피곤한 길에서

of *the two Flanders and of Brabant. He had been born
두 플란다스와 브라반트의.   파트라슈는 태어났다

/ to no other heritage / than those of pain and of toil. He
물려받은 것도 없이   고통과 힘든 일 외에는.

had been fed on curses / and baptized with blows. Why
욕을 먹이 삼아   매질 세례를 받으며 자랐다.   왜 아니었겠는

not? It was a Christian country, / and Patrasche was but
가?   그곳은 기독교 국가였고,   파트라슈는 그저 개였을 뿐이었다.

a dog. Before he was fully grown / he had known / the
파트라슈는 완전히 자라기도 전에   알게 되었다

bitter gall of the cart and the collar. Before he had entered
짐수레와 목줄의 쓰라린 아픔을.   파트라슈가 13개월이 채 되기 전에

his thirteenth month / he had become the property of a
철물상의 소유가 되었다.

hardware-dealer, / who was accustomed to / wander over
그는 익숙한 사람이었다

the land north and south, / from the blue sea / to the green
북쪽과 남쪽으로 떠돌아 다니는데,   푸른 바다로부터   녹색 산들까지.

mountains. They sold him for a small price, / because he
그들은 헐값에 파트라슈를 팔았다,   왜냐하면 파트라슈는

was so young.
매우 어렸기 때문에.

* 동플란다스와 서플란다스를 일컬음

alpha and omega 시작과 끝 | treasury 금고 | granary 창고 | wand 마법의 지팡이 | bread-winner 생계비를
벌어 오는 사람 | comforter 위안을 주는 사람 | hide 털, 가죽 | limb 다리 | bowed 활처럼 휘다 | wring
쥐어짜다, 괴롭히다 | toil 힘써 일하다 | cruelly 잔혹한 | sire 조상 | shaft (복수)수레 손잡이 | harness 마구 |
sinews (복수형으로) 근육, 체력 | gall 피부가 쓸려서 벗겨지다 | breaking one's heart 비통하게 만들다 | flint 돌
| weary 지치게 하는 | baptize 세례를 주다 | collar 개 목걸이 | property 소유 | hardware-dealer 철물상 |
be accustomed to ~에 익숙한 | wander 헤메이다

15

This man was a drunkard / and a brute. The life of
새 주인은 술고래에다가   짐승같은 사람이었다.

Patrasche was / a life of hell. To deal the tortures of hell
파트라슈의 인생은   마치 지옥같았다.   지옥같은 고통을 주는 것은

/ on the animal creation / is a way / which the Christians
동물에게   한 방법이었다   기독교인들이 갖고 있는

have / of showing their belief in it. His purchaser was /
자신들의 신앙심을 표현하는.   파트라슈를 산 사람은

a sullen, ill-living, brutal Brabantois, / who heaped his
무뚝뚝하고 고약했으며 난폭한 브라반트 사람이었는데,   짐수레에 가득 실었다

cart full / with pots and pans and flagons and buckets, /
취사 도구와 큰 병과 양동이와,

and other wares of crockery and brass and tin, / and left
다른 집기와 놋쇠와 주석으로 된 그릇들을,

Patrasche to draw the load / as best he might, / whilst he
그리고 파트라슈에게 그 짐을 끌게 했다   할 수 있는 한 많이,

himself lounged idly / by the side / in fat and sluggish ease,
자신은 한가로이 서성이면서,   곁에서   느릿느릿 편하게 움직였다,

/ smoking his black pipe / and stopping / at every wineshop
검은색 파이프 담배를 피우거나   들르면서   모든 술집과 카페에

or café / on the road.
길가에 있는.

drunkard 술고래 | brute 짐승 | sullen 무뚝뚝한 | ill-living 고약한 | brutal 난폭한 | heap 수북하게 쌓다 |
flagon 큰 병 | crockery 집기 | brass 놋쇠 | lounge 서성이다 | sluggish 느릿느릿 움직이다 | travail 고생 |
lash 채찍질 | agony 고통 | saunter 빈둥거리다, 한가로이 걷다 | quiver 떨다

Happily for Patrasche / —— or unhappily —— / he was very
파트라슈에게 다행인지   — 혹은 불행인지 —   매우 튼튼했다:

strong: / he came of an iron race, / long born and bred / to
무쇠같은 핏줄을 타고 태어나서,   오랫동안 길러졌다

such cruel travail; / so that he did not die, / but managed to
그런 잔혹한 고역 속에서;   그래서 죽지는 않았지만,   다만 견뎌낼 뿐이었다

/ drag on a wretched existence / under the brutal burdens, /
비참한 삶을 질질 끄는 것을   잔혹하고 무거운 짐 아래서,

the scarifying lashes, / the hunger, the thirst, the blows, the
채찍질을 당하고,   배고픔과, 목마름, 구타와 욕설, 그리고 탈진을 경험하면서

curses, and the exhaustion / which are the only wages / with
이런 것들만이 유일한 보수였다

which the Flemings repay / the most patient and laborious
플란다스 사람들이 보답해 준   가장 인내심 강하고 일 잘하는

/ of all their four-footed victims. One day, / after two years
그들의 모든 네 발 달린 피해자들에게.   하루는,   2년이 지난 후

/ of this long and deadly agony, / Patrasche was going on /
이런 길고 살인적인 고통의 삶이 시작된지,   파트라슈는 가는 중이었다

as usual / along one of the straight, dusty, unlovely roads
평상시처럼   쭉 뻗고, 먼지 나는 좋지 않은 길을 따라

/ that lead to the city of Rubens. It was full midsummer, /
루벤스 시로 이어지는.   때는 한여름이었고,

and very warm. His cart was very heavy, / piled high with
매우 더웠다.   그의 짐수레는 매우 무거웠다,   상품들이 높이 쌓여서

goods / in metal and in earthenware. His owner sauntered
금속과 토기로 된.   그의 주인은 빈둥거렸다

on / without noticing him / otherwise / than by the crack
파트라슈를 신경 쓰지 않고   안 그랬다면   채찍이 날아와서

of the whip / as it curled round his quivering loins. The
파트라슈의 떨리는 허리를 휘감았을 것이다.

Brabantois had paused / to drink beer himself / at every
브라반트 사람은 잠시 멈춰 서서   맥주를 마셨다   길가의 술집이

wayside house, / but he had forbidden Patrasche / to stop a
나타날 때마다,   하지만 파트라슈에게는 못 하게 했다   잠시 멈추는 것도

moment / for a draught from the canal. Going along thus,
물 한 모금 마시기 위해.   이렇게 걸어가면서,

/ in the full sun, / on a scorching highway, / having eaten
쟁쟁 내리쬐는 태양 아래,   타는 듯한 길에서   하루 종일 아무것도 먹지

nothing / for twenty-four hours, / and, / which was far
못한 채   24시간 동안,   그리고,   그보다 더 심한 것은,

worse to him, / not having tasted water / for near twelve,
                혀 한 번 축이지 못하고   거의 12시간 째,

/ being blind with dust, / sore with blows, / and stupefied
먼지로 뒤덮인 채,   매질을 당하며,

with the merciless weight / which dragged upon his loins, /
무자비한 무게에 마비되어 버렸다   허리에 걸쳐져 끌리는,

Patrasche staggered / and foamed a little at the mouth, / and
그래서 파트라슈는 휘청거리며   입에 거품을 물고,

fell.
쓰러졌다.

He fell / in the middle of the white, dusty road, / in the full
파트라슈는 쓰러졌다   하얗고 먼지 날리는 길 한가운데에,

glare of the sun; / he was sick unto death, / and motionless.
햇볕이 쏟아지는;   그는 죽을 듯이 아팠고,   움직임이 없었다.

His master gave him / the only medicine in his pharmacy
그의 주인은 주었다   가지고 있던 단 하나의 약을

/ —— kicks and oaths / and blows with a cudgel of oak, /
    — 바로 발로 차고 욕설을 하며   오크 나무로 만든 곤봉으로 때리는,

which had been often the only food and drink, / the only
그것들은 유일한 식사와 음료였고,

wage and reward, / ever offered to him. But Patrasche
유일한 임금이고 보상이었다.   그에게 주어지는.   하지만 파트라슈는 넘어선

was beyond / the reach of any torture or of any curses.
곳에 있었다   고통이나 어떤 욕설도 닿을 수 없는.

Patrasche lay, / dead to all appearances, / down in the white
파트라슈는 누워 있었다. 죽은 듯이,   하얀 가루를 뒤집어 쓰고

powder / of the summer dust. After a while, / finding it
        여름철 먼지의.   잠시 후,   소용없음을 알게 되자

useless / to assail his ribs with punishment / and his ears
            갈비뼈를 걷어 차는 처벌이나

scorching 모든 것을 태워 버릴 듯이 더운 | stupefy 망연자실 하다 | merciless 무자비한 | stagger 휘청거리다 |
foam 거품을 물다 | oath 욕설 | cudgel 곤봉 | torture 고문 | assail 공격을 가하다

with maledictions, / **the Brabantois** / —— deeming / **life**
귀에 악담을 하는 것이,　브라반트 사람은　—— 생각하면서　

gone in him, / **or going so nearly** / **that his** carcass **was**
그가 죽었다고,　또는 거의 죽어서　시체도 전혀 쓸모 없고,

forever useless, / **unless indeed** / **someone should strip**
　만약 정말로　누군가 그 개의 가죽을 벗거나 하지 않

it of the skin / **for gloves** —— / cursed **him** fiercely / **in**
는다면　장갑을 만들려고 —　지독한 욕설을 퍼붓고

farewell, / **struck off the leathern bands of the harness,** /
작별 인사로,　굴레의 가죽 끈을 잘라내고,

kicked his body / **aside into the grass,** / **and,** / groaning
몸을 발로 차서　풀밭으로 밀어낸 후,　그리고,

and muttering / **in** savage wrath, / **pushed the cart lazily**
짜증내고 투덜거리며　몹시 화가 나서,　짐수레를 느리게 밀었다

/ **along the road up-hill,** / **and left the dying dog** / **for the**
　오르막 길을 따라서,　죽어가는 개를 내버려 두고

ants to sting / **and for the crows to pick.**
개미들이 뜯어먹고　까마귀들이 쪼아대도록.

maledictions 저주 | deeming ~으로 여기다 | fiercely 사납게 | groan 짜증을 내다, 신음 소리를 내다 | mutter 투덜거리다 | savage 사나운 | wrath 분노 | sting 쏘다

It was the last day / before Kermesse away at Louvain, /
그 날은 마지막 날이었다,　　　루뱅에서 축제일의 장이 열리는,

and the Brabantois was in haste / to reach the fair / and get
그래서 브라반트 사람은 서둘렀다　　　축제에 도착하여

a good place / for his truck of brass wares. He was in fierce
좋은 자리를 잡으려고　놋쇠 그릇을 팔기 위한.　　　그는 매우 화를 냈다,

wrath, / because Patrasche had been a strong / and much-
왜냐하면 파트라슈는 튼튼했고　　　상당히 인내심 많은

enduring animal, / and because he himself / had now the
동물이었기 때문에,　　그리고 그 자신이　　　이제는 어려운 일을

hard task / of pushing his charette / all the way to Louvain.
맡았기 때문에　그의 수레를 끌어야 하는　　　루뱅에 도착할 때까지.

But / to stay to look after Patrasche / never entered his
하지만　파트라슈를 돌보기 위해서 머무르는 것은　　전혀 생각도 하지 않았다:

thoughts: / the beast was dying and useless, / and he would
　　그 짐승은 죽어가고 있었으며 쓸모가 없으니,　　　그는 도둑질을 할 참이

steal, / to replace him, / the first large dog / that he found
었다,　파트라슈를 대신하기 위해,　처음 만나는 큰 개를　　혼자 서성이고 있는 것을

wandering alone / out of sight of its master. Patrasche had
발견하면　　　주인의 눈 밖에서.　　　파트라슈는 아무 비용도

cost him nothing, / or next to nothing, / and for two long, /
들지 않았고,　　　혹은 거의 공짜나 다름없었다,　그리고 2년 동안,

cruel years / had made him toil ceaselessly / in his service
잔인한 세월인　쉴 틈 없이 부려먹었다　　자신을 위해서

/ from sunrise to sunset, / through summer and winter, / in
해 뜰 때부터 해 질 때까지,　　　여름이든 겨울이든,

fair weather and foul.
날씨가 좋든 나쁘든.

Key Expression 🎵

cost A B: A에게 B의 비용(희생)을 치르게 하다
cost가 '비용이 들다'라는 의미로 쓰일 때 비용을 치르는 대상을 알리고 싶은 경우
'cost + 대상 + 비용'의 형태인 4형식 문장을 사용합니다.

ex) Patrasche had cost him nothing.
파트라슈는 그에게 아무 댓가도 치르게 하지 않았다. (→파트라슈는 공짜로 일했다)

20　A Dog of Flanders

He had got a fair use / and a good profit out of Patrasche:
파트라슈는 제법 쓸모가 있었고 파트라슈로 인해 돈도 벌었다:

/ being human, / he was wise, / and left the dog / to draw
사람이었기에, 그는 영리했고, 개를 내버려 두었다

his last breath / alone in the ditch, / and have his bloodshot
마지막 숨을 거두도록 홀로 배수로에서, 그리고 핏발이 선 눈이 뽑히도록

eyes plucked out / as they might be by the birds, / whilst he
새들에 의해,

himself went on his way / to beg and to steal, / to eat and
한편 자신은 가던 길을 갔다 구걸하고 훔치고, 먹고 마시며,

to drink, / to dance and to sing, / in the mirth at Louvain.
춤추고 노래하기 위해서, 루뱅 축제에서.

A dying dog, / a dog of the cart / —— why should he waste
죽어가는 개, 짐 수레를 끄는 개 따위는 — 그가 시간을 허비할 이유가 될까

hours over its agonies / at peril of losing a handful of
한 줌의 동전을 잃는 손해를 감수하고,

copper coins, / at peril of a shout of laughter?
즐거운 시간을 희생하며?

Patrasche lay there, / flung in the grass-green ditch. It
파트라슈는 그곳에 누워 있었다, 초록빛 풀이 무성한 배수로로 내던져진 채.

was a busy road that day, / and hundreds of people, / on
그날은 길이 혼잡했고, 수백 명의 사람들이,

foot and on mules, / in wagons or in carts, / went by, /
걷거나 노새를 타고, 우마차나 짐수레를 타고, 지나갔다,

tramping quickly and joyously / on to Louvain. Some saw
빠르고 즐거운 걸음으로 루뱅으로 향했다. 몇몇은 파트라슈를

him, / most did not even look: / all passed on. A dead dog /
보았지만, 대부분은 쳐다보지도 않았다: 모두가 지나쳤다. 죽은 개는

more or less / —— it was nothing / in Brabant: / it would be
기껏해야 — 대단한 일이 아니었다 브라반트에서는: 그리고 아무 일도

nothing / anywhere in the world.
아닐 것이다 세계 어느 곳에서도.

---

ceaseless 끊임없는 | ditch 배수로 | bloodshot 핏발이 선 | mirth 웃음 소리 | peril 위험 | mule 노새 | tramp
타박 타박 걷다

A. 다음 문장을 해석해 보세요.

(1) Patrasche came of a race / which had toiled hard and cruelly / from sire to son / in Flanders / many a century.
→

(2) To deal the tortures of hell / on the animal creation / is a way / which the Christians have / of showing their belief in it.
→

(3) Patrasche to draw the load / as best he might, / whilst he himself lounged idly / by the side / in fat and sluggish ease.
→

(4) His owner sauntered on / without noticing him / otherwise than by the crack of the whip / as it curled round his quivering loins.
→

B. 다음 주어진 문장이 되도록 빈칸에 써 넣으세요.

(1) 그들은 결코 <u>우연이라도</u> 풍족했던 적이 없다.

They never _____ had enough.

(2) 파트라슈가 죽거나 그들 곁을 떠난다면, <u>그들 자신도 몸져 누워서 같은 식으로 죽었을 것이다</u>.

Patrasche dead or gone from them, _____
_____ .

(3) 파트라슈는 <u>고통과 힘든 일 외에는 물려받은 것이 없이</u> 태어났다.

He had been born to _____
_____ .

A. (1) 파트라슈는 플란다스에서 수백 년 동안 대대로 힘들게 일했고 학대받아온 종족으로부터 태어났다. (2) 동물에게 지옥같은 고통을 주는 것은 기독교인들이 자신들이 가지고 있는 신앙심을 표현하는 한 방법이었다. (3) 파트라슈에게 할 수 있는 한 많은 짐을 끌게 하고, 그 자신은 곁에서 한가로이 서성이면서 느릿

(4) 그는 <u>욕을 먹고 매질 세례를 받아왔다.</u>

He had been [   ].

C. 다음 주어진 문구가 알맞은 문장이 되도록 순서를 맞추어 보세요.

(1) 파트라슈는 아무 비용도 들지 않았고, 혹은 거의 공짜나 다름없었다.
(had cost / Patrasche / nothing, / or / next to / him / nothing)
→

(2) 파트라슈는 <u>초록빛 풀이 무성한 배수로에 내던져진 채</u> 그 곳에 누워 있었다.
(in / grass-green / the / ditch / flung)
Patrasche lay there, [   ].

(3) 그것은 세계 어느 곳에서도 아무 일도 아닐 것이다.
(in / It / nothing / the world / anywhere / would be)
→

(4) 파트라슈는 <u>어떤 고문이나 욕설도 닿을 수 없는 곳에</u> 있었다.
(or / the reach / any torture / of / of / any curses / beyond)
Patrasche was [   ]
[   ].

D. 다음 단어에 대한 맞는 설명과 연결해 보세요.

(1) impious   ▶   ◀ ① work very hard

(2) trample   ▶   ◀ ② lack of respect for religious

(3) toil   ▶   ◀ ③ step heavily

(4) agony   ▶   ◀ ④ great physical or mental pain

느릿 편하게 움직였다. (4) 그의 주인은 파트라슈를 전혀 신경 쓰지 않고 빈둥거렸고 그렇지 않으면 채찍으로 파
트라슈의 떨리는 허리를 휘감았다. | B. (1) by any chance (2) they must have laid themselves down and died
likewise (3) no other heritage than those of pain and of toil (4) fed on curses and baptized with blows | C. (1)
Patrasche had cost him nothing, or next to nothing. (2) flung in the grass-green ditch (3) It would be nothing
anywhere in the world. (4) beyond the reach of any torture or of any curses | D. (1) ② (2) ③ (3) ① (4) ④

2

After a time, / among the holiday-makers, / there came a
한참 뒤,　　　　명절을 즐기러 가는 사람들 사이로,　　키가 작은 할아버지

little old man / who was bent and lame, and very feeble.
한 분이 왔다　　구부정하고 절름발이에 매우 허약한.

He was in no guise for feasting: / he was very poorly and
그는 축제를 위한 차림이 아니었다:　　　그는 매우 가난하고 초라한 차림이었고,

miserably clad, / and he dragged his silent way / slowly /
　　　　　조용히 발걸음을 옮겼다　　　　천천히

through the dust / among the pleasure-seekers. He looked
먼지를 뚫고　　즐기는 사람들 사이를.　　　　그는 파트라슈를

at Patrasche, / paused, wondered, / turned aside, / then
쳐다보고,　　잠시 멈춰서서 의아해하며　　옆으로 돌아섰다.

kneeled down / in the rank grass and weeds of the ditch,
그런 다음 무릎을 꿇고　풀과 잡초가 무성한 배수로 위에,

/ and surveyed the dog / with kindly eyes of pity. There
개를 살폈다　　　동정심이 담긴 다정한 눈길로.

was with him / a little rosy, / fair-haired, / dark-eyed child
그의 곁에는 있었다　　발그레한 볼과,　　금발 머리에,　　짙은 눈동자를 가진 아이가

/ of a few years old, / who pattered / in amidst the bushes,
두세 살 쯤 된,　　　　아이는 토닥토닥 걸어와 수풀 한복판에서,

/ for him breast-high, / and stood gazing / with a pretty
가슴까지 오는,　　　　선 채 바라보았다　　꽤 진지한 눈길로

seriousness / upon the poor, great, quiet beast.
　　　　　불쌍하고, 커다랗고, 조용한 짐승을.

Thus / it was that these two first met / —— the little Nello
이렇게 하여　그 둘이 처음 만나게 되었다

and the big Patrasche.
— 어린 넬로와 커다란 파트라슈가.

The upshot of that day was, / that old Jehan Daas, / with
그 날 결국,　　　　　　　예한 다스 할아버지는,

much laborious effort, / drew the sufferer homeward / to
힘들게 애쓴 끝에,　　　　고통 받고 있는 그 짐승을 집으로 끌고 왔다

holiday-maker 명절을 즐기러 가는 사람, 행락객 | feeble 허약한 | guise 가장, 겉모습 | feast 축제, 연회 | clad (옷)
을 입은 | pleasure-seeker 흥미거리를 찾는 사람, 행락객 | kneel down 무릎을 꿇다 | patter 토닥토닥 소리를 내다
| upshot 결말 | laborious 힘든 | tawny 황갈색의 | harsh 가혹한 | soothe 달래다

his own little hut, / which was a stone's throw off / amidst
그의 작은 오두막으로,　　　　　바로 코 앞에 있던

the fields, / and there / tended him / with so much care
들판 한가운데에,　그리고 거기에서　그를 돌봤다　　온 정성을 다하여

/ that the sickness, / which had been a brain seizure, /
　그래서 그 병은,　　　　뇌졸중이었던,

brought on by heat and thirst and exhaustion, / with time
열기와 탈수 그리고 탈진으로 생긴,　　　　　　　　시간을 들여 그늘에서

and shade and rest / passed away, / and health and strength
휴식을 취한 후　　　　사라졌고,　　　　건강과 기운이 되돌아 와서,

returned, / and Patrasche staggered up again / upon his four
파트라슈는 비틀거리며 걸을 수 있게 되었다

stout, tawny legs.
튼튼한 황갈색의 네 다리로.

Now for many weeks / he had been useless, / powerless,
여러 주 동안　　　　　　　　그는 아무 쓸모도 없었고,　　기운이 없고, 아파서,

sore, / near to death; / but all this time / he had heard no
　거의 죽을 뻔 했다;　하지만 그 모든 시간 동안　파트라슈는 전혀 욕설을

rough word, / had felt no harsh touch, / but only the pitying
듣지 않았고,　　가혹한 매질도 당하지 않았다,　다만 불쌍히 여기는 속삭임과

murmurs / of the child's voice / and the soothing caress / of
　　　　　어린 아이의　　　　　달래며 어루만지는 손길뿐이었다

the old man's hand.
할아버지의.

In his sickness / they too had grown to care for him, / this
파트라슈가 앓는 동안   그들도 파트라슈를 돌보는데 익숙해졌다.

lonely man and the little happy child. He had a corner of
외로운 할아버지와 행복한 어린 아이는.   파트라슈는 오두막의 구석을

the hut, / with a heap of dry grass / for his bed; / and they
차지했다.   마른 풀을 쌓아 올려   그의 잠자리로;

had learned to listen eagerly / for his breathing / in the
그리고 그들은 열심히 귀담아 듣게 되었다   파트라슈의 숨소리를

dark night, / to tell them that he lived; / and when he first
어두운 밤이면,   파트라슈가 살아있음을 알려 주는;   그리고 파트라슈가 충분히

was well enough to essay / a loud, hollow, broken bay, /
건강해져서 처음으로 짖었을 때,   크고, 맥없이 갈라지는 소리로,

they laughed aloud, / and almost wept together for joy / at
그들은 큰 소리로 웃었고,   동시에 기쁨으로 거의 울 뻔 했다

such a sign of his sure restoration; / and little Nello, / in
파트라슈가 완전히 회복한 기색을 보고;   그리고 넬로는,

delighted glee, / hung round his rugged neck / with chains
너무 기쁘고 신이 나서,   상처투성이인 파트라슈의 목에 매달려

of *marguerites, / and kissed him / with fresh and ruddy
마거리트 색의 줄이 그어진,   입을 맞췄다   생기 있고 발그레한 입술로.

lips.

So then, / when Patrasche arose, himself again, / strong,
그렇게 해서,   파트라슈가 스스로 다시 일어났을 때,   튼튼하고,

big, gaunt, powerful, / his great wistful eyes / had a gentle
크고, 수척하지만, 건장한 모습으로, 그의 애석함이 담긴 큰 눈에는

astonishment in them / that there were no curses to rouse
그들에 대한 은근한 놀람이 있었다   자신에게 일어나려는 욕설도 없고

him / and no blows to drive him; / and his heart awakened
재촉하는 매질도 없는 것에;   그래서 그의 마음이 열렸다

/ to a mighty love, / which never wavered once / in its
그 크나큰 사랑에,   한 번도 흔들린 적 없었던   신의에 있어서

fidelity / whilst life abode with him.
그가 살아온 삶 동안.

* 마거리트-데이지와 비슷한 국화과의 꽃. 여기서는 꽃 색과 비슷한 상처 자국을 의미

But Patrasche, / being a dog, / was grateful. Patrasche lay
비록 파트라슈는, 개였지만, 감사해 했다. 파트라슈는 누워서

pondering long / with grave, tender, musing brown eyes, /
오랫동안 생각했다 의젓하고, 부드럽고, 사려 깊은 갈색눈으로,

watching the movements of his friends.
친구들의 행동을 바라보면서.

Now, / the old soldier, / Jehan Daas, / could do nothing /
이제는, 전직 군인이었던, 예한 다스는, 할 수 있는 것이 없었다

for his living / but limp about a little / with a small cart,
생계를 위해 절뚝거리며 걸어다니는 것 말고는 작은 수레를 끌고,

/ with which / he carried daily / the milk-cans of those
그 수레를 그는 매일 끌고 다녔다 그보다 조금 더 행복한 이웃들의 우유병들을

happier neighbors / who owned cattle away / into the town
소를 소유하고 있는 안트베르펜 마을까지.

of Antwerp. The villagers gave him the employment / a
마을 사람들이 그에게 일자리를 주었다

little out of charity / —— more because it suited them well
선심을 써서 — 하지만 더 큰 이유는 그게 더 좋았기 때문이다

/ to send their milk into the town / by so honest a carrier, /
우유를 도시로 보내고 정직한 운반원을 통해서,

and bide at home themselves / to look after their gardens,
자신들은 집에 머물면서 정원을 돌보거나,

/ their cows, their poultry, / or their little fields. But it was
젖소와 닭, 오리를, 또는 밭을 돌보는 것이.

becoming hard work / for the old man. He was eighty-
하지만 일이 점점 힘들어지고 있었다 할아버지에게는. 그는 여든 세 살이었고,

three, / and Antwerp was / a good league off, or more.
안트베르펜은 족히 5Km 쯤, 또는 그 이상 떨어진 곳이었다.

Patrasche watched the milk-cans come and go / that one
파트라슈는 우유통이 오가는 것을 보았다 어느 날

day / when he had got well / and was lying in the sun / with
그가 건강해져서 햇빛을 쐬고 있을 때

the wreath of marguerites / round his tawny neck.
마거리트 화환같은 상처가 황갈색 목에 남아있는 채.

heap 더미 | eagerly 열심히 | bay 짖다 | restoration 회복 | glee 신남 | rugged 다부진 | gaunt 수척한 |
wistful 애석해 하는 | rouse 자극하다 | waver 흔들리다 | fidelity 성실, 충실 | abide·머물다 | ponder 곰곰이
생각하다 | grave 수수한 | muse 사색하다 | poultry 닭, 오리, 거위 따위의 가금류 | wreath 화환

The next morning, / Patrasche, / before the old man had
다음 날 아침,   파트라슈는,   할아버지가 수레에 손도 대기 전에,

touched the cart, / arose and walked to it / and placed
일어나서 수레 쪽으로 걸어가서

himself betwixt its handles, / and testified / as plainly / as
수레 손잡이 사이에 몸을 집어넣고,   표현했다   분명히

dumb show could do / his desire and his ability to work /
몸짓으로 최대한   일하고 싶다는 바람을

in return for the bread of charity / that he had eaten. Jehan
음식과 선의에 대한 보답으로   자신이 받았던.

Daas resisted long, / for the old man was one of those / who
예한 다스는 한참동안 반대했다, 왜냐하면 할아버지는 그런 사람이었다

thought it a foul shame / to bind dogs to labor / for which
부끄러운 일이라고 생각하는   일을 시키려고 개를 묶는 것을

Nature never formed them. But Patrasche / would not be
대자연의 뜻을 거스르는 일이기에.   하지만 파트라슈는   들으려 하지 않았다:

gainsaid: / finding they did not harness him, / he tried to
그들이 자신에게 마구를 채우지 않는다는 것을 알고,

draw the cart onward / with his teeth.
파트라슈는 수레를 끌려고 시도했다   자신의 이빨로 물어서.

Key Expression ♀

so that : ~하기 위해서

so that이 이끄는 절이 조동사(주로 can)를 동반할 때에는 '~하기 위하여, ~하
도록'이라고 해석합니다. 이때 so that은 in order that으로 바꿀 수 있어요.

ex) He fashioned his cart so that Patrasche could run in it.
    그는 파트라슈가 끌 수 있도록 짐수레를 고쳤다.

betwixt 사이에 | testify 증언하다 | plainly 분명히 | dumb show 몸짓, 무언극 | foul 좋지 않은 | Nature
대자연 | gainsay 반대하다 | vanquish 완파하다 | persistence 끈기, 고집 | gratitude 감사 | succor 구조 |
thenceforward 그때부터 | rut 바퀴 자국 | frightful 끔찍한 | compel 강요하다

At length / Jehan Daas gave way, / vanquished / by the
결국   예한 다스는 포기했다,   완전히 압도되어

persistence and the gratitude / of this creature whom he
그 끈기와 감사하는 마음에   그가 구해낸 이 동물의.

had succored. He fashioned his cart / so that Patrasche
그는 수레마차를 고쳤다   파트라슈가 끌 수 있도록,

could run in it, / and this he did / every morning of his life
그리고 파트라슈는 수레를 끌었다   평생동안 매일 아침

/ thenceforward.
그날 이후로.

When the winter came, / Jehan Daas thanked the blessed
겨울이 다가오자,   예한 다스는 행운에 감사해 했다

fortune / that had brought him / to the dying dog in the
그 자신을 데려간   배수로에서 죽어가는 개에게

ditch / that fair-day of Louvain; / for he was very old, /
루뱅 축제일에;   왜냐하면 그는 매우 늙었고,

and he grew feebler / with each year, / and he would ill
점점 더 연약해졌기 때문에   해마다,   그는 알지 못했을 것이었다

have known / how to pull his load of milk-cans / over the
우유통 수레를 어떻게 끌어야 할지

snows / and through the deep ruts in the mud / if it had
눈길 위에서   진흙탕에 깊이 빠진 바퀴를

not been / for the strength and the industry of the animal /
만약 없었다면   파트라슈의 힘과 근면함이

he had befriended. As for Patrasche, / it seemed heaven to
그의 친구가 되어 준.   하지만 파트라슈에게는,   천국과 같았다.

him. After the frightful burdens / that his old master had
그 끔찍했던 짐을 끌었던 이후라서   예전 주인이 강요하여

compelled him / to strain under, / at the call of the whip at
혹사당했던,   발을 뗄 때마다 채찍질을 맞으며,

every step, / it seemed nothing to him but amusement / to
그에게는 다만 즐겁기만 했다

step out / with this little light green cart, / with its bright
나가는 일이   작고 가벼운 녹색 수레를 끌고,   밝은 색의 놋쇠통을 실은,

brass cans, / by the side of the gentle old man / who always
다정한 할아버지의 곁에서   언제나 파트라슈에게

paid him / with a tender caress / and with a kindly word.
보답해 주는   부드러운 손길과   상냥한 말로.   29

Besides, / his work was over by three or four in the day,
뿐만 아니라, 일은 오후 서너 시면 끝났고,

/ and after that time / he was free to do as he would / ——
그 이후에는 하고 싶은 일을 마음대로 할 수 있었다

to stretch himself, / to sleep in the sun, / to wander in the
— 기지개를 펴거나, 햇볕 아래에서 잠을 자거나, 들판을 돌아다니며,

fields, / to romp with the young child, / or to play with his
어린 아이와 뛰어 놀았고, 또는 다른 개들과 놀기도 했다.

fellow-dogs. Patrasche was very happy.
파트라슈는 매우 행복했다.

Fortunately / for his peace, / his former owner was killed /
운 좋게도 파트라슈의 평화를 위해서인지, 그의 전 주인은 죽었다

in a drunken brawl / at the *Kermesse of *Mechlin, / and
술에 취해 싸우다가 메헬렌의 축제일 장터에서,

so sought not after him / nor disturbed him / in his new
그래서 파트라슈를 찾거나 방해하는 일은 없었다

and well-loved home.
새로운 집에서 사랑받으며 살고 있는.

A few years later, / old Jehan Daas, / who had always
몇 년 후, 예한 다스 할아버지는, 항상 절뚝거렸던,

been a cripple, / became so paralyzed with rheumatism /
류마티즘으로 마비가 심해져

that it was impossible for him / to go out with the cart any
더 이상 할 수 없게 되었다 수레를 끌고 나가는 일을.

more. Then / little Nello, / being now grown to his sixth
그러자 어린 넬로가, 이제 여섯 살이 되었지만,

year of age, / and knowing the town well / from having
도시를 잘 알고 있는 할아버지와 같이 다녀서

accompanied his grandfather / so many times, / took his
여러 차례,

place beside the cart, / and sold the milk / and received
할아버지 대신 수레 옆에 서서, 우유를 팔고

the coins in exchange, / and brought them back / to their
대가로 동전을 받아, 가져다 주었다

* 네덜란드 등의 지방의 축제일에 열리는 장
** 벨기에의 도시

respective owners / with a pretty grace and seriousness /
각 주인들에게   성실하고 진지하게,

which charmed all who beheld him.
그 행동은 그를 지켜본 모든 사람들의 호감을 샀다.

romp 뛰어 놀다 | brawl 싸움 | paralyze 마비시키다 | respective 각각의 | charm 호감을 사다 | behold
지켜보다

The little Ardennois / was a beautiful child, / with dark,
아르덴 소년은   예쁜 아이였다,

grave, tender eyes, / and a lovely bloom upon his face, / and
짙고 깊은 부드러운 눈동자와,   사랑스러운 홍조를 띈 얼굴에,   금발

fair locks / that clustered to his throat; / and many an artist
곱슬 머리를 지녔다 목 주변에서 찰랑거리는;   그래서 많은 예술가들이 둘의 모

sketched the group / as it went by him / —— the green cart /
습을 그렸다   그들이 곁을 지날 때면   — 녹색 수레와,

with the brass flagons / of Teniers and Mieris and Van Tal, /
큰 놋쇠병을 실은   테니르 씨와 미리스 씨와 반 탈 씨의,

and the great tawny-colored, massive dog, / with his belled
거대한 황갈색의 개와,

harness that chimed cheerily / as he went, / and the small
목줄에 달린 종이 울리는 소리를 내는   지나갈 때면,   그리고 어린 아이의 모습은

figure / that ran beside him / which had little white feet /
그 옆을 달려가는   작고 하얀 발에

in great wooden shoes, / and a soft, grave, innocent, happy
커다란 나막신을 신고,   부드럽고, 의젓하고, 순수하며, 행복한 얼굴을 한

face / like the little fair children of Rubens.
루벤스의 그림에 나오는 어린 아이들처럼.

Nello and Patrasche did the work so well / and so joyfully
넬로와 파트라슈는 맡은 일을 잘했고   함께 즐거워하며 일했다

together / that Jehan Daas himself, / when the summer
그래서 예한 다스는,   여름이 돌아오고

Key Expression

as good as : ~와 다름없는

as good as는 '~와 다름없는' 혹은 '사실상'이라는 의미를 가진 관용표현입니다.
같은 뜻을 가진 표현으로 no better than를 사용하기도 합니다.

ex) Anyway, there is greenery and breadth of space enough to be as good as
beauty to a child and a dog.
어쨌든, 아이와 개에게는 충분히 아름다운 푸른 자연과 넓은 공간이 있었다
The hut was scarce better than a shed when the nights were cold.
그 오두막은 추운 밤에는 가축 우리나 다름없었다.

bloom 홍조를 띠다 | cluster 다발지다 | massive 거대한 | chime 울다 | wicket 문 | doze 선잠을 자다, 꾸벅
꾸벅 졸다 | recount 이야기하다 | rye 호밀 | twilight 땅거미 | veil 가리우다 | burgh 도시 | colza 평지 |
pasture 초원 | plough 쟁기 | succeed 계속되다 | characterless 개성 없는

came / and he was better again, / had no need to stir out,
다시 건강을 되찾았을 때, 움직일 필요가 없었고,

/ but could sit in the doorway / in the sun / and see them
문가에 앉아 있기만 했다 햇볕 아래 그리고 그들이 가는 것을

go forth / through the garden wicket, / and then doze and
보았다 정원의 문을 지나서, 그리고 나서 선잠에 빠져 꿈을 꾸거나

dream / and pray a little, / and then awake again / as the
기도를 하기도 했다. 그러다가 다시 깨어나서

clock tolled three / and watch for their return. And on their
시계가 3시를 치면 그들이 돌아오는 것을 지켜보곤 했다. 그리고 그들이

return / Patrasche would shake himself / free of his harness
돌아오면 파트라슈는 몸을 떨곤 했다 끈을 풀어주어 자유가 된 기쁨에,

with a bay of glee, / and Nello would recount / with pride
그리고 넬로는 이야기 하곤 했다

the doings of the day; / and they would all go in together
그날 한 일을 자랑스러워 하며; 그리고 모두 함께 집 안으로 들어가

/ to their meal of rye bread and milk or soup, / and would
호밀로 만든 빵과 우유 또는 수프로 차려진 식사를 하고, 지켜보곤 했다

see / the shadows lengthen / over the great plain, / and see
그림자가 길어지는 것을 넓은 들판 위로,

the twilight veil the fair cathedral spire; / and then lie down
또 땅거미가 성당의 첨탑을 가리는 것을 보았고;

together / to sleep peacefully / while the old man said a
그리고 나서 같이 누워서 평안하게 잠을 청했다 할아버지가 기도를 하는 동안에.

prayer. So the days and the years went on, / and the lives of
그렇게 하루하루, 한 해 두 해 세월이 흘렀고,

Nello and Patrasche were / happy, innocent, and healthful. In
넬로와 파트라슈의 삶은 행복하고, 순수하고, 건강했다.

the spring and summer / especially were they glad. Flanders
봄과 여름에는 넬로와 파트라슈는 특히 즐거워했다. 플란다스는

is not a lovely land, / and around the burgh of Rubens / it
그렇게 아름다운 곳이 아니었고, 루벤스의 유적 주변은

is perhaps least lovely of all. Corn and colza, / pasture and
아마 가장 초라한 곳일지도 모른다. 옥수수밭과 들판, 초원과 쟁기들이,

plough, / succeed each other / on the characterless plain /
계속해서 이어질 뿐이었다 아무 특징도 없는 평야에

in wearying repetition, / and save by some gaunt gray
지루하게 반복되는, 수척한 회색 탑들을 빼면,

tower, / with its peal of pathetic bells, / or some figure
애처로운 종소리를 울리는,

coming athwart the fields, / made picturesque / by a
또는 어떤 이가 들판을 가로질러 오는 모습이, 그림같은 모습을 만들어 내는 것 외에

gleaner's bundle / or a woodman's fagot, / there is no
이삭 줍는 사람들의 무리나 나뭇꾼의 장작더미가, 아무 변화도

change, / no variety, no beauty / anywhere; / and he who
없었고, 화려함이나 아름다움이 없었다 아무데도; 살아봤던 사람이라면

has dwelt / upon the mountains / or amidst the forests /
산 위나 숲속에서

feels oppressed / as by imprisonment / with the tedium
우울함을 느끼는 법이다 갇힌 듯 단조롭게 끝없이 펼쳐진

and the endlessness / of that vast and dreary level. But it
거대하고 황량한 지평선에.

is green and very fertile, / and it has wide horizons / that
하지만 그 땅은 푸르고 매우 비옥했으며, 넓은 지평선이 있었다

have a certain charm of their own / even in their dulness
그 나름의 매력을 갖고 있는 그런 지루하고 단조로움 속에서도;

and monotony; / and among the rushes / by the water-
골풀 사이에선 물가의

side / the flowers grow, / and the trees rise tall and fresh
꽃들이 피어났고, 나무들도 크고 싱싱하게 자랐다

/ where the barges glide / with their great hulks black /
바지선들이 물 위를 지나갔고 선체가 검은 색으로 보이는

against the sun, / and their little green barrels / and vari-
태양을 등진 탓에, 배 안의 녹색 통들과

colored flags / gay against the leaves. Anyway, / there is
가지각색의 깃발들은 나뭇잎과 대비되어 아름다웠다. 어찌됐든,

greenery and breadth of space / enough to be as good as
그곳에는 푸른 자연과 넓은 공간이 있었다 충분히 아름다운

beauty / to a child and a dog; / and these two asked no
아이와 개에게는; 그리고 이 둘은 더 이상 바라지 않았다,

better, / when their work was done, / than to lie buried
일이 끝나면, 울창한 풀밭 위에 파묻히든 누워서

in the lush grasses / on the side of the canal, / and watch
운하 곁에 있는,

the cumbrous vessels drifting by / and bring the crisp salt
큰 배가 떠가는 것을 바라보았다   그러면 바다의 산뜻한 소금 냄새가 밀려

smell of the sea / among the blossoming scents / of the
왔다   막 피어나는 꽃 향기에 섞여

country summer.
이곳의 여름에.

True, / in the winter / it was harder, / and they had to rise /
사실,   겨울에는   더욱 힘들었다.   그들은 일어나야 했고

in the darkness and the bitter cold, / and they had seldom
어둠과 혹된 추위 속에서,   거의 가져보지 못했다

/ as much as they could have eaten / any day, / and the hut
제대로 먹을 수 있을 만큼   그 어떤 날도,

was scarce better than a shed / when the nights were cold,
또한 오두막은 가축 우리나 마찬가지였다   추운 밤에는,

/ although it looked so pretty / in warm weather, / buried
그러나 무척 아름다웠다   따뜻한 계절에는,

in a great kindly clambering vine, / that never bore fruit,
무성하게 감싸는 포도 넝쿨에 파묻혀,   열매를 맺은 적이 없지만,

/ indeed, / but which covered it / with luxuriant green
실제로,   포도 넝쿨은 오두막을 뒤덮었다   화려한 초록빛 그물처럼

tracery / all through the months of blossom and harvest.
꽃이 피고 수확하는 계절 내내.

In winter / the winds found many holes / in the walls of
겨울에는   수많은 구멍으로 바람이 불어왔다   초라하고 작은 오두막의

the poor little hut, / and the vine was black and leafless, /
벽에 있는,   그리고 포도 넝쿨은 잎사귀도 없이 검게 말라 버렸으며,

and the bare lands looked very bleak and drear without, /
텅 빈 마당은 황량하고 을씨년스러워 보였다.

repetition 반복 | peal 종소리 | pathetic 애처로운 | athwart 가로질러 | picturesque 그림같은 | gleaner 이삭
줍는 사람 | fagot 장작 더미 | oppress 억압 받다 | imprisonment 감금 | tedium 지루함 | dreary 음울한 |
fertile 비옥한 | dulness 따분함 | monotomy 단조로움 | rush 골풀, 등심초 | barge 바지선 | glide 미끄러지다
| hulk 선체 | barrel 통 | vari-colored 여러 색의 | greenery 녹색 나뭇잎 | lush 울창한 | cumbrous 큰,
거대한 | drift 이동하다 | crisp 상쾌한 | bitter 모진, 살을 에는 듯한 | clambering 기어오르다 | tracery 창 장식,
그물무늬 | bleak 황폐한, 쓸쓸한 | drear (시어=dreary), 황량한, 처량한

and sometimes / within the floor / was flooded and then
그리고 때로는 / 집 안의 바닥도 / 물이 흥건하여 이내 얼어붙었다.

frozen. In winter / it was hard, / and the snow numbed /
겨울에는 / 정말 힘들었고, / 눈은 꽁꽁 얼어붙게 했으며

the little white limbs of Nello, / and the icicles cut / the
넬로의 작고 흰 팔다리를, / 고드름은 상처를 냈다

brave, untiring feet of Patrasche.
파트라슈의 용감하고, 지칠 줄 모르는 발에.

But even then / they were never heard to lament, / either
그럼에도 불구하고 / 그들은 불평하는 적이 없었다.

of them. The child's wooden shoes / and the dog's four
둘 중 누구도. / 아이의 나막신과 / 개의 네 다리는

legs / would trot manfully together / over the frozen
/ 씩씩하게 함께 걸어갔다 / 언 땅 위를

fields / to the chime of the bells on the harness; / and then
/ 가죽 끈에 달린 방울 소리에 맞추어;

sometimes, / in the streets of Antwerp, / some housewife
그러면 때로는, / 안트베르펜 거리에서, / 어떤 아주머니가 그들에게

would bring them / a bowl of soup and a handful of
갖다 주곤 했다 / 수프 한 그릇과 빵 한 덩어리를.

bread, / or some kindly trader would throw / some billets
/ 또는 어떤 마음씨 좋은 상인이 넣어주기도 했다 / 장작 몇 덩이를

of fuel / into the little cart / as it went homeward, / or
/ 작은 수레 안에 / 집으로 향할 때,

some woman in their own village / would bid them / keep
또는 마을에 사는 어떤 부인은 / 그들에게 제의하기도 했다

a share of the milk / they carried for their own food; / and
우유를 조금 가져가라고 / 자신들의 식량으로 들고 가던;

they would run over the white lands, / through the early
그러면 이들은 새하얀 땅 위를 달려서, / 초저녁의 어둠을 뚫고,

darkness, / bright and happy, / and burst / with a shout of
밝고 행복하게, / 뛰어들었다 / 기쁨의 함성을 지르며

joy / into their home.
/ 집 안으로.

numb (추위 등으로 인해) 마비시키다, 감각을 잃게 하다 | icicle 고드름 | untiring 지치지 않는, 불굴의 | even then 그럼에도 불구하고 | lament 한탄하다 | trot 총총걸음으로 가다, 속보로 걷다 | manfully 남자답게, 씩씩하게 | billet 막대기, 장작 | homeward 집으로

 mini test 2

A. 다음 문장을 해석해 보세요.

(1) When he first was well enough to essay / a loud, hollow, broken bay, / they laughed aloud, / and almost wept together for joy / at such a sign of his sure restoration.
→

(2) Jehan Daas resisted long, / for the old man was one of those / who thought it a foul shame / to bind dogs to labor / for which Nature never formed them.
→

(3) They had seldom / as much as they could have eaten / any day, / and the hut was scarce better than a shed / when the nights were cold.
→

(4) But even then / they were never heard to lament, / either of them.
→

B. 다음 주어진 문구가 알맞은 문장이 되도록 순서를 맞춰보세요.

(1) 예한 다스는 작은 수레를 끌고 절뚝거리며 다니는 것 말고는 생계를 위해 할 수 있는 게 없었다.
(but / do / his / could / for / nothing / living)
Jehan Daas _____ limp about a little with a small cart.

(2) 그는 파트라슈가 그 안에 들어가 끌 수 있도록 수레를 고쳤다.
(fashioned / in / He / could run / Patrasche / his cart / it / so that)
→

 Answer

A. (1) 그가 충분히 건강해져서 처음으로 맥없이 갈라지는 소리로 크게 짖었을 때, 그들은 완전히 회복한 기색을 보고 크게 웃으며 기뻐서 거의 울 뻔했다. (2) 예한 다스는 오랫동안 반대했다. 왜냐하면 할아버지는 일을 시키기 위해 개를 묶는 것은 대자연의 뜻을 거스르는 부끄러운 일이라고 생각했기 때문이다. (3)

38 A Dog of Flanders

(3) 이 가벼운 녹색 수레를 끌고 나가는 것은 그에게 단지 즐겁기만 했다.
(but / nothing / seemed / It / amusement / to him)

to step out
with this little light green cart.

(4) 그 이후에는 그가 하고 싶은 대로 자유롭게 할 수 있었다.
(as / he was / to / he would / do / free)
After that time

C. 다음 주어진 문장이 본문의 내용과 맞으면 T, 틀리면 F에 동그라미 하세요.

(1) Patrasche had been near to death, but finally came to recover.
[T / F]

(2) Patrasche replaced the old man for pushing his cart.
[T / F]

(3) People in the village were not kind to Nello's family.
[T / F]

(4) Flanders is a very beautiful land and the burgh of Rubens is the best.
[T / F]

D. 의미가 서로 비슷한 것끼리 연결해 보세요.

(1) bay ▶   ◀ ① muse
(2) ponder ▶   ◀ ② tedious
(3) persistence ▶ ◀ ③ bark
(4) weary ▶   ◀ ④ resolution

 3

So, / on the whole, / it was well with them, / very well; /
따라서, 전반적으로, 그들은 행복했다. 정말 좋았다;

and Patrasche, / meeting on the highway or in the public
그리고 파트라슈는, 큰길이나 거리에서 만나면서

streets / the many dogs / who toiled from daybreak into
많은 개들을 새벽부터 한밤중까지 애써 일하고도,

nightfall, / paid only with blows and curses, / and loosened
구타와 욕설만 당하는, 겨우 풀려난

/ from the shafts / with a kick / to starve and freeze as best
그 고통으로부터 버려지고 나서야 굶주리고 꽁꽁 얼어버린 채

they might / — Patrasche / in his heart / was very grateful
— 파트라슈는 마음 속으로 그의 운명에 깊이 감사했고,

to his fate, / and thought it / the fairest and the kindliest /
생각했다 가장 온당하고 친절한 운명이라고

the world could hold. Though he was often very hungry
세상에서 가질 수 있는. 비록 무척 배고플 때도 정말 많았고

indeed / when he lay down at night; / though he had to
밤에 잠자리에 들면; 일을 해야 했지만

work / in the heats of summer noons / and the rasping chills
여름철 한낮의 뙤약볕 아래와 겨울 새벽의 에는 듯한 추위 속에서;

of winter dawns; / though his feet were often tender / with
또한 발도 자주 아팠지만

wounds / from the sharp edges of the jagged pavement; /
상처로 인해 울퉁불퉁한 길의 날카로운 바닥 때문에 입은;

though he had to perform tasks / beyond his strength and
그리고 맡은 일을 해야 했지만 그의 체력을 넘어서고 힘에 부치는

against his nature / — yet he was grateful and content: /
— 그렇지만 그는 감사했고 행복했다:

he did his duty / with each day, / and the eyes that he loved
그는 맡은 일을 했다 매일 매일, 그리고 그가 사랑하는 이의 눈길이

/ smiled down on him. It was sufficient for Patrasche.
미소지으며 그를 바라보았다. 파트라슈는 그것만으로도 충분했다.

---

shaft 거칠고 불공정한 대우 | rasping 거친 | tender 아프다 | uneasiness 불편함 | gateway 길목 | taverns
선술집 | swell 높은 음 | peal 울리다 | sanctuary 성소 | squalor 불결함 | stagnant 잔잔한

There was only one thing / which caused Patrasche any
단 한 가지가 있었다   파트라슈의 삶에 불안을 주는 일이,

uneasiness in his life, / and it was this. Antwerp, / as all the
                  그건 바로 이것이었다.   안트베르펜은,

world knows, / is full / at every turn / of old piles of stones, /
전 세계가 알고 있듯,   가득하다   모퉁이마다   오래된 석조물들이,

dark and ancient and majestic, / standing in crooked courts,
어두운 색의 오래되고 장엄한,   구불구불한 골목에 서 있거나,

/ jammed against gateways and taverns, / rising by the
선술집 사이에 웅기종기 모여 있거나,   강가 옆에 우뚝 솟아 있었다,

water's edge, / with bells ringing above them in the air, / and
                  종소리가 하늘 높이 울려 퍼지고,

ever and again out of their arched doors / a swell of music
또 아치 모양의 문 밖으로   고조된 음악 소리가 울려 나오는.

pealing. There they remain, / the grand old sanctuaries of
         그곳에 있다,   위대하고 유서 깊은 오래된 성지들이,

the past, / shut in / amidst the squalor, the hurry, the crowds,
그 과거의,   차단된 채   현실 세계의 불결함과, 분주함, 북적대는 사람들, 추함,

the unloveliness, / and the commerce of the modern world,
                  그리고 장삿속 판치는 한가운데에,

/ and all day long the clouds drift / and the birds circle / and
그리고 온종일 구름이 떠다니고   새들이 맴돌며

the winds sigh around them, / and beneath the earth at their
바람이 한 숨을 쉬는 곳에,   그리고 그들의 발 아래 땅 속에

feet / there sleeps / —— RUBENS.
그곳에 잠자고 있다   — 루벤스가.

And the greatness of the mighty Master / still rests upon
그리고 대단한 거장의 위대함은   여전히 안트베르펜에 깃들어 있다,

Antwerp, / and wherever we turn / in its narrow streets /
                  그리고 우리가 어디로 향하건   그 좁은 골목에서

his glory lies therein, / so that all mean things are thereby
그의 영광이 그곳에 존재하여,   모든 초라한 것들이 그로 인해 변했다;

transfigured; / and as we pace slowly / through the winding
                  그리고 우리가 천천히 걸어가면   구불구불한 골목을 지나,

ways, / and by the edge of the stagnant water, / and through
잔잔한 물가를,

41

the noisome courts, / his spirit abides with us, / and the
그리고 악취가 나는 광장을 지나갈 때, 그의 정신이 우리와 함께하며,

heroic beauty of his visions is about us, / and the stones /
그의 비전의 웅대한 아름다움이 우리를 에워싸고, 돌들은

that once felt his footsteps and bore his shadow / seem to
한 때 그의 발자국을 느꼈고 그의 그림자가 드리웠던

arise and speak of him / with living voices. For the city
일어나 그에 대해 이야기 하는 듯 하다 살아있는 목소리로. 왜냐하면 그 도시는

/ which is the tomb of Rubens / still lives to us / through
  루벤스가 묻힌 곳인 우리에게는 아직도 살아있기 때문이다

him, / and him alone.
그를 통해, 오직 그 한 사람을 통해.

It is so quiet there / by that great white sepulcher / ——
그곳은 무척 조용하다 웅장하고 흰 무덤 주위는

so quiet, / save only when the organ peals / and the choir
— 너무나 조용하다, 오르간 소리가 울릴 때와 성가대가 노래할 때를

cries aloud / *the Salve Regina or **the Kyrie Eleison.
제외하곤 '여왕이시여'나 '주여 불쌍히 여기소서'를.

Sure / no artist ever had a greater gravestone / than that
확실히 그 어떤 예술가도 가지지 못했다 더 큰 비석을

pure marble sanctuary gives to him / in the heart of his
순 대리석으로 된 성소가 그에게 준 것보다 그가 태어난 곳의 중심에 자리한

birthplace / in the chancel of St. Jacques.
  성자크 성당에 마련된.

Without Rubens, / what were Antwerp? A dirty, dusky,
루벤스가 없다면, 안트베르펜은 무슨 의미가 있을까? 지저분하고, 음침하고,

bustling mart, / which no man would ever care to look
북적거리는 시장은, 아무도 거들떠 보지 않을 것이다

upon / save the traders / who do business on its wharves.
  상인들을 제외하곤 부둣가에서 장사를 하는.

With Rubens, / to the whole world of men / it is a sacred
루벤스가 있기에, 전 세계 모든 사람들에게 그곳은 성스러운 이름이요,

name, / a sacred soil, / a Bethlehem where a god of Art
성스러운 땅이다, 예술의 신이 빛을 본 베들레헴이며,

saw light, / a Golgotha where a god of Art lies dead.
  예술의 신이 잠든 골고다이다.

* (성가) 여왕이시여
** (성가) 주여 불쌍히 여기소서

O nations! / Closely should you treasure your great men, /
오 전 세계 나라들이여! 그대들의 위대한 인물들을 보배롭게 여길지어다.

for by them alone / will the future know of you. Flanders
왜냐하면 오직 그들을 통해   미래가 그대의 나라를 기억할테니.   플란다스 사람들은

/ in her generations / has been wise. In his life / she
대대로   현명했다.   루벤스가 살아있을 때

glorified / this greatest of her sons, / and in his death / she
플란다스는 칭송했고 이곳이 낳은 가장 위대한 인물을,   그가 죽자

magnifies his name. But her wisdom is very rare.
그의 이름을 찬미한다.   하지만 이렇게 현명한 일은 지극히 드문 것이다.

noisome 불쾌한 | abide 머무르다 | sepulcher 무덤, 묘 | choir 성가대 | dusky 음침한, 어둑한 | bustling
분주한 | wharf 부두 | treasure 소중히 여기다

Now, / the trouble of Patrasche was this. Into these great,
그때, 파트라슈를 괴롭히는 일은 이것이었다.   이러한 웅장하면서도 슬퍼

sad piles of stones, / that reared their melancholy majesty
보이는 석조물 안으로,   구슬픈 왕을 세운

/ above the crowded roofs, / the child Nello would many
다닥다닥 붙어 있는 지붕들 위로,   어린 넬로는 수없이 들어가서,

and many a time enter, / and disappear through their dark
어두운 아치형 입구 속으로 사라지곤 했다,

arched portals, / whilst Patrasche, / left without upon the
그 동안 파트라슈는,   길 위에 홀로 남겨져,

pavement, / would wearily and vainly ponder / on what
지루해 하며 헛된 생각에 빠지곤 했다

could be the charm / which thus allured / from him / his
매혹하는 것이 무엇일까에 대해   그렇게 데려가 버리는   자신으로부터

inseparable and beloved companion. Once or twice / he
뗄 수 없는 사랑스런 단짝을.   한두 번

did essay to see for himself, / clattering up the steps /
직접 보려고 시도했다,   덜거덕거리는 소리를 내며 계단을 올라

with his milk-cart behind him; / but thereon / he had been
우유가 들린 수레를 뒤에 맨 채;   하지만 그 즉시,   항상 뒤로 내몰렸다

always sent back again summarily / by a tall custodian /
키 큰 관리인에 의해

in black clothes and silver chains of office; / and fearful of
검은 색 줄이 달린 검은 제복을 입은;

bringing his little master into trouble, / he desisted, / and
그러면 어린 주인에게 피해를 줄까 봐,   단념하고,

remained couched / patiently / before the churches / until
웅크린 채 기다렸다   참을성 있게   성당 앞에서

such time as the boy reappeared. It was not the fact of his
소년이 다시 나타날 때까지.   그가 그곳에 들어간다는 사실은 아니었다

going into them / which disturbed Patrasche: / he knew /
파트라슈를 괴롭힌 것은;   파트라슈도 알고 있었다

that people went to church: / all the village went / to the
사람들이 성당에 다닌 다는 것은: 마을의 모든 이들이 갔으니까

small, tumbledown, gray pile / opposite the red windmill.
작고, 허물어질 듯한, 회색 석조물로   빨간 풍차 건너편에 있는.

What troubled him / was that little Nello always looked
그를 걱정스럽게 한 것은   어린 넬로는 이상한 표정을 짓는 것이었다

strangely / when he came out, / always very flushed or
          그가 나왔을 때면,   항상 매우 상기되어 있거나 매우 창백했다;

very pale; / and whenever he returned home / after such
그리고 집에 돌아갈 때면   이러한 방문 이후

visitations / would sit silent and dreaming, / not caring to
          조용히 앉아서 공상에 잠기곤 했다,   놀려고 하지도 않고,

play, / but gazing out at the evening skies / beyond the line
저녁 하늘을 멍하니 바라보며   운하 저 너머를,

of the canal, / very subdued and almost sad.
          매우 침울하여 슬퍼 보이기까지 하는 표정으로.

Key Expression ❣

부정어를 이용한 최상급 표현

최상급은 형용사 뒤에 est를 붙이거나 형용사 앞에 most를 사용하는 것이 일반적이지만, 부정주어와 함께 비교급 및 원급을 사용해서도 최상급을 표현할 수 있습니다. 다양한 최상급 표현 방법을 알아볼까요.

▶ 부정주어 ~ 비교급 + than ~
 = 부정주어 ~ so + 원급 + as ~
 = 긍정주어 ~ 비교급 + than + any other + 단수명사
           anyone/anything else

ex) No artist ever had a greater gravestone than that pure marble sanctuary
   gives to him.
   어떤 예술가도 대리석 성소가 그에게 준 것보다 더 위대한 비석을 가지지 못했다
   (=대리석 성소에 있는 그의 비석이 예술가 중에서 가장 위대하다)

thereon 그 즉시 | summarily 즉석에서, 즉시 | custodian 관리인 | desist 단념하다, 그만두다 | couch 웅크리다,
쭈그리다 | tumbledown 무너질 듯한, 황폐한 | windmill 풍차 | flushed 홍조를 띤 | subdue 가라앉히다.
차분하게 하다

45

What was it? / wondered Patrasche. He thought / it could
무엇일까? 파트라슈는 궁금해 했다. 그는 생각했다 그것이 좋은 일

not be good or natural / for the little lad to be so grave, /
이나 자연스러운 일은 아닐 것이라고 어린 소년에게 그토록 침통한 표정을 짓게 하니,

and in his dumb fashion / he tried all he could / to keep
그래서 말을 못 하는 상황에서 할 수 있는 일은 모두 해 보았다

Nello by him / in the sunny fields / or in the busy market-
넬로를 곁에 두려고 햇살이 가득한 들판이나 분주한 장터로 데리고 나가서.

place. But to the churches / Nello would go: / most often
하지만 성당으로 넬로는 가려 했다: 대부분

of all / would he go to the great cathedral; / and Patrasche,
성모 대성당으로 가려 했다: 그리고 파트라슈는,

/ left without on the stones / by the iron fragments of *
돌바닥에 홀로 남겨진 채 퀜틴 마시스의 철제 문 옆에,

Quentin Matsys's gate, / would stretch himself / and yawn
기지개를 켜고 하품을 하며 한숨

and sigh, / and even howl / now and then, / all in vain, /
을 쉬며, 윙윙 짖기도 했다 이따금, 하지만 모두 헛수고였다,

until the doors closed / and the child perforce came forth
문이 닫히고 아이는 어쩔 수 없이 다시 밖으로 나오자,

again, / and winding his arms about the dog's neck / would
그러면 개의 목에 팔을 두르고

kiss him on his broad, tawney-colored forehead, / and
그의 넓은 황갈색 이마에 입을 맞추며,

murmur always the same words: / "If I could only see
항상 똑같은 말을 중얼거렸다: "그것들을 볼 수만 있다면,

them, / Patrasche! / —— if I could only see them!"
파트라슈! — 그것들을 볼 수만 있다면!"

What were they? / pondered Patrasche, / looking up / with
그것들은 무엇이었을까? 파트라슈는 곰곰이 생각했다, 위를 쳐다보며

large, wistful, sympathetic eyes.
크고, 안타깝고, 동정 어린 눈으로.

---

* 플란다스 지방의 화가 퀜틴 마시스(1466~1530)

howl 짖다 | now and then 때때로, 이따금 | perforce 부득이 | leave ajar (문이) 조금 열어 두다 | rapt 넋을
잃은, 정신이 팔린 | ecstasy 황홀, 희열 | altar-picture 제단화 | Assumption (성화) 성모 승천 | into the air
바깥으로, 야외로

One day, / when the custodian was out of the way / and
하루는, 관리인이 자리에 없을 때

the doors left ajar, / he got in for a moment / after his little
문이 살짝 열려 있어서, 파트라슈는 잠시 안으로 들어가 보았다 어린 친구를 따라

friend / and saw. "They" were two great covered pictures /
그리고 보았다. "그것들"은 가려진 두 점의 웅장한 그림이었다

on either side of the choir.
성가대의 양 편에 걸려 있는.

Nello was kneeling, / rapt as in an ecstasy, / before the
넬로는 무릎을 꿇고 있었다, 황홀함에 빠져,

altar-picture of the Assumption, / and when he noticed
성모 승천을 그린 제단화 앞에. 그리고 파트라슈가 온 것을 보고,

Patrasche, / and rose and drew the dog gently out into
일어나서 개를 살그머니 끌고 밖으로 나왔다,

the air, / his face was wet with tears, / and he looked up
그의 얼굴은 눈물로 흠뻑 젖어 있었고, 가려진 그림을 올려다 보면서

at the veiled places / as he passed them, / and murmured
그것을 지나칠 때,

to his companion, / "It is so terrible not to see them, /
그의 친구에게 속삭였다, "볼 수 없다니 너무해,

Patrasche, / just because one is poor / and cannot pay! He
파트라슈, 가난해서 돈을 낼 수 없다는 이유만으로!

never meant / that the poor should not see them / when he
그분은 의도하지 않았을 거야 가난한 사람들이 그림을 보면 안 된다고

painted them, / I am sure. He would have had us see them
저 그림들을 그렸을 때, 난 확신해. 그분은 우리에게 보여 주셨을 거야

/ any day, every day: / that I am sure. And they keep them
언제든, 매일: 확실히 그럴 거야. 그런데 사람들은 저곳에 그림을

shrouded there / —— shrouded in the dark, / the beautiful
가려 두었어 — 어두운 곳에 가리둔 거야, 저렇게 아름다운 것들

things! / —— and they never feel the light, / and no eyes
을! — 그래서 그림들은 절대로 빛을 볼 수 없고 아무도 그림들을 볼 수

look on them, / unless rich people come and pay. If I could
없어, 부자들이 와서 돈을 내지 않는 한.

only see them, / I would be content to die."
그것들을 볼 수만 있다면, 죽어도 좋을 텐데."

But / he could not see them, / and Patrasche could not help
하지만 그는 볼 수 없었고, 파트라슈는 그를 도와줄 수 없었다,

him, / for to gain the silver piece / that the church exacts /
왜냐하면 은화를 얻는 것은 성당이 요구하는

as the price for looking on / the glories of *the Elevation
보는 값으로

of the Cross and **the Descent of the Cross / was a thing
'십자가에 매달림'과 '십자가에서 내리심'의 영광을

as utterly beyond the powers of either of them / as it would
둘의 능력을 한참 벗어나는 일이었기 때문에

have been to scale / the heights of the cathedral spire.
오르는 것 만큼이나 성당의 뾰족탑의 높이를.

They had never so much as a sou to spare: / if they cleared
그들은 한 푼이라도 여유돈을 가져본 적이 없었다: 만약 살 수 있도록 충분

enough to get / a little wood for the stove, / a little broth
하다면 난로에 땔 약간의 장작을, 혹은 냄비에 끓일 약간의

for the pot, / it was the utmost / they could do. And yet /
수프를, 그게 최선이었다 그들이 할 수 있는. 하지만

the heart of the child was set in / sore and endless longing /
아이의 마음은 꽂혀 있었다 지독하고 끊임없는 갈망에

upon beholding the greatness of the two veiled Rubens.
루벤스의 두 점의 위대한 작품을 보려는.

The whole soul of the little Ardennois / thrilled and stirred
작은 아르덴 소년의 온 마음은 전율하고 요동쳤다

/ with an absorbing passion for Art. Going on his ways
예술에 대한 열렬한 열정으로. 오래된 도시를 지날 때

through the old city / in the early days / before the sun or
이른 새벽에 태양도 사람들도 일어나기 전,

the people had risen, / Nello, / who looked only a little
넬로는, 그저 작은 시골 소년으로 보이는,

peasant-boy, / with a great dog / drawing milk to sell from
큰 개와 함께 집집마다 팔기 위해 우유를 끄는,

door to door, / was in a heaven of dreams / whereof Rubens
꿈 속의 천국에 가 있었다 루벤스가 신으로 있는.

was the god. Nello, / cold and hungry, / with stockingless
넬로는, 춥고 배고팠지만, 양말도 신지 않은 채

* (성화) 십자가에 매달림
** (성화) 십자가에서 내리심

feet / in wooden shoes, / and the winter winds blowing
나막신을 신고,   겨울 바람이 그의 곱슬 머리를 흩날리고

among his curls / and lifting his poor thin garments, / was
애처롭도록 얇은 그의 옷자락을 들어 올렸지만,

in a rapture of meditation, / wherein all that he saw / was
상상 속에서 환희에 차 있었다,   그 속에서 오로지 보이는 것은

the beautiful fair face / of the Mary of the Assumption,
아름답고 고운 얼굴 뿐이었다   승천하는 성모 마리아의,

/ with the waves of her golden hair lying / upon her
금발 머리의 물결이 찰랑거리고   어깨 위에서,

shoulders, / and the light of an eternal sun / shining down
영원한 태양빛이   얼굴을 비추이고 있는

upon her brow. Nello, / reared in poverty, / and buffeted by
모습이.   넬로는,   가난 속에서 자라,   운명과 싸웠고,

fortune, / and untaught in letters, / and unheeded by men, /
글을 배우지도 못했으며,   사람들에게 무시당했지만,

had the compensation or the curse / which is called Genius.
그에 대한 보상 혹은 저주를 받은 것이다   천재라는 이름의.

Key Expression 🍀

with를 사용한 부대상황 구문

부대상황이란 두 가지 일이 동시에 일어날 때를 표현하는 구문으로, 다음처럼 네 가지 형태로 표현할 수 있으며 '~를 ~하면서' 혹은 '~를 ~한 채로'라고 해석합니다. 보통 분사를 사용할 경우에는 '~를 ~하면서', 형용사나 전치사구를 사용할 경우에는 '~ 를 ~한 채로라고 해석하면 됩니다.

▶ with + 목적어 + 현재분사
▶ with + 목적어 + 과거분사
▶ with + 목적어 + 형용사 ~을 ~한 채로
▶ with + 목적어 + 전치사구 ~을 ~한 채로

ex) …with a great dog drawing milk to sell from door to door, …
…커다란 개에게 각 집에서 나온 팔 우유를 끌게 하면서, …
…with his milk-cart behind him. …우유 수레를 뒤에 둔 채.
…with stockingless feet in wooden shoes, …맨발로 나막신을 신은 채,

exact 요구하다 | utterly 아주 | stir 요동하다 | absorbing 열정적인, 열렬한 | stockingless 맨발의 |
rapture 큰 기쁨 | wherein 그 중에서(in which와 동의어) | buffet 싸우다 | unteach in letters 글을 모르다 |
compensation 보상, 대가

No one knew it. He as little as any. No one knew it. Only
아무도 그 사실을 몰랐다. 넬로 또한 몰랐다. 아무도 알지 못했다.

indeed Patrasche, / who, / being with him always, / saw
다만 파트라슈만 알았다, 파트라슈는, 그와 항상 함께 있으면서, 보았고

/ him draw with chalk / upon the stones / any and every
그가 석필로 그리면 돌 위에

thing that grew or breathed, / heard / him on his little bed of
그 모든 그림이 살아나 숨쉬는 것을, 들었으며 그가 작은 지푸라기 침대에서

hay / murmur / all manner of timid, / pathetic prayers / to
중얼거리는 것을 수줍어하는 태도로, 애처롭게 기도하며

the spirit of the great Master; / watched / his gaze darken
전능하신 하나님께; 또한 보았다 그의 눈빛이 어두워지고

and / his face radiate / at the evening glow of sunset / or the
그의 얼굴이 빛을 발하는 것을 해질녘 저녁 놀에

rosy rising of the dawn; / and felt / many and many a time
또는 장밋빛으로 밝아오는 새벽녘에; 그리고 느꼈다 수없이 여러 번

/ the tears of a strange, nameless pain and joy, / mingled
이상야릇하고 이름 모를 아픔과 기쁨의 눈물이, 서로 뒤엉켜,

together, / fall hotly / from the bright young eyes / upon his
뜨겁게 떨어지는 것을 소년의 맑은 두 눈에서

own wrinkled yellow forehead.
자신의 주름진 누런 이마 위로.

Key Expression 🔑

now and then : 때로는

now and then은 '때로는, 때때로'의 의미로 every now and then이라고
도 합니다. 같은 의미로 쓰이는 다양한 표현으로 다음과 같은 표현들이 있습니다.

▶ sometimes, occasionally / on occasion / (every) once in a while / at times /
from time to time / (every) now and then

ex) Patrasche would stretch himself and yawn and sigh, and even howl now and
then. 파트라슈는 때로는 기지개를 켜고 한숨을 쉬며 왕왕 짖기도 했다.

* 루벤스와 반다이크를 뒤따르는 17세기 플랑드르의 중심 작가
** 15세기 네덜란드의 화가 형제
*** 유럽 서부 프랑스·벨기에·네덜란드를 흐르는 강
**** 파리에서 남동쪽에 있으며 1179년부터 1477년까지 부르고뉴공국의 수도였음
***** 그리스 신화의 트로이 전쟁의 영웅

hay 지푸라기 | pathetic 애처로운, 안쓰러운 | radiate 빛을 발하다 | mingle 섞다 | hotly 뜨겁게 | couldst (고어)
can의 2인칭 단수 과거형 | Baas 주인님, 나리 | ideal 이상 | deem 생각하다 | leaven 기운, 빚어내는 힘, 원동력 |
divinity 거룩함, 신성함

"I should go to my grave quite content / if I thought, /
"무덤에서 편히 잠들 수 있을 텐데   만약,

Nello, / that when thou growest a man / thou couldst own
넬로야,   네가 어른이 되었을 때

this hut and the little plot of ground, / and labor for thyself,
이 오두막과 조그만 땅 덩어리를 가지고,   자신을 먹여 살릴 수 있고,

/ and be called Baas / by thy neighbors," / said the old man
나리라고 불릴 수 있다면   이웃 사람들에게,"   예한 할아버지는 말했다

Jehan / many an hour / from his bed. For to own a bit of
여러 번   침대에 누운 채.   왜냐하면 땅을 소유하고,

soil, / and to be called Baas / — master — / by the hamlet
나리라고 불리는 것이   — 지주라는 뜻의 —   주변에서,

round, / is to have achieved / the highest ideal of a Flemish
이룬 것을 의미하기 때문이다   플란다스 농부들의 최고의 이상을;

peasant; / and the old soldier, / who had wandered over all
그리고 이 늙은 군인은,   전 세계를 떠돌다

the earth / in his youth, / and had brought nothing back, /
젊은 시절에,   빈손으로 돌아왔기에,

deemed / in his old age / that to live and die / on one spot
생각했던 것이다   나이가 들어서   살다가 생을 마치는 것이   한 곳에서

/ in contented humility / was the fairest fate / he could
소박한 삶에 만족하며   최선의 운명이라고   그가 바랄 수 있는

desire / for his darling. But Nello said nothing.
사랑하는 손자를 위해.   하지만 넬로는 아무 말도 하지 않았다.

The same leaven was working / in him / that in other times
똑같은 기운이 움직이고 있었다   그의 안에는   과거 다른 시대에

/ begat / Rubens and *Jordaens and **the Van Eycks, /
만들어 냈던   루벤스와 요르단스와 반 에이크,

and all their wondrous tribe, / and in times more recent
그리고 모든 위대한 거장들을,   그리고 더 최근에는

/ begat / in the green country of the Ardennes, / where
만들어 냈던   아르덴의 푸른 시골에서,

***the Meuse washes / the old walls of ****Dijon, / the
뫼즈 강이 씻어내고   디종의 낡은 절벽을,

great artist / of *****the Patroclus, / whose genius is / too
위대한 예술가를   파트로클로스를 그린,   이들의 천재성은   너무

near us / for us / aright to measure / its divinity.
가까이 있어   우리로서는   가늠하기 힘든 법이다   그 신성함을.   51

Nello dreamed of other things / in the future / than of
넬로는 다른 일들을 꿈꾸었다   미래에 대해

tilling the little ***rood** of earth, / and living under the
작은 땅 덩어리를 경작하거나,   나뭇가지로 엮은 지붕 밑에 살며,

wattle roof, / and being called Baas / by neighbors / a little
나라라 불리는 것과는 다른   이웃에게

poorer or a little less poor than himself. The cathedral
자신보다 좀 더 가난하거나 덜 가난한.   성당의 뾰족탑은,

spire, / where it rose beyond the fields / in the ruddy
들판 너머로 솟아오른   붉게 물든 저녁 하늘에

evening skies / or in the dim, gray, misty mornings, / said
또는 어둑한, 잿빛의, 안개 낀 아침에,   그에게

other things to him / than this. But these / he told only
다른 꿈들을 말해 주었다   이것과는 다른. 하지만 이들을   그는 파트라슈에게만

to Patrasche, / whispering, / childlike, / his fancies / in
이야기 했다,   속삭이며,   아이처럼,   그의 꿈들을

the dog's ear / when they went together / at their work /
개의 귓가에 대고   그들이 함께 갈 때나   일터에

through the fogs of the daybreak, / or lay together at their
새벽 안개를 가르며,   또는 함께 누워 쉴 때

rest / among the rustling rushes / by the water's side.
    바스락거리는 골풀들 사이에   강가에서.

For such dreams / are not easily shaped into speech / to
왜냐하면 그런 꿈들은   쉽게 말로 표현할 수 없으니까

awake the slow sympathies / of human auditors; / and
공감을 불러일으키기도록   듣는 사람들의;

they would only / have sorely perplexed and troubled /
그리고 단지   몹시 어리둥절하고 당황스럽게 만들테니까

the poor old man / bedridden in his corner, / who, for his
가난한 노인을   방 한구석에 몸져 누워 지내는,   할아버지의 경우,

part, / whenever he had trodden the streets of Antwerp, /
    안트베르펜 거리를 걸을 때마다,

had thought the daub of blue and red / that they called a
파란색과 빨간색의 칠 범벅이라 생각했었다   사람들이 성모마리아라고 부르는

---

* 토지 면적의 단위, 1acre의 ¼, 약 1,011.7㎡, 약 300평

Madonna, / on the walls of the wine-shop / where he drank
그림도,　　　술집 벽에 걸려 있는

his sou's worth of black beer, / quite as good / as any of the
한 푼어치의 흑맥주를 마셨던,　　　그다지 다를 게 없었다

famous altar-pieces / for which the stranger folk / travelled
그 어느 유명한 제단화라도　　　이방인인 그에게는

far and wide / into Flanders / from every land / on which
여러 곳을 떠돌다가　　플란다스까지 들어온　어디든지 다니다가

the good sun shone.
햇빛이 잘 비추이는 곳이면.

tilly 갈다, 경작하다 | wattle 나뭇가지를 엮어 흙으로 바른 | sorely 몹시 | perplexed 어리둥절한 | bedrid 몸져
눕다 | daub 더덕더덕 칠함 | Madonna 성모마리아 | sou 한 푼

 mini test 3

A. 다음 문장을 해석해 보세요.

(1) There they remain, / the grand old sanctuaries of the past, / shut in / amidst the squalor, the hurry, the crowds, the unloveliness, / and the commerce of the modern world.
→

(2) The greatness of the mighty Master / still rests upon Antwerp, / and wherever we turn / in its narrow streets / his glory lies therein, / so that all mean things are thereby transfigured.
→

(3) For the city / which is the tomb of Rubens / still lives to us / through him, / and him alone.
→

(4) What troubled him / was that little Nello always looked strangely / when he came out, / always very flushed or very pale.
→

B. 다음 주어진 문장이 되도록 빈칸에 써 넣으세요.

(1) 루벤스가 없다면, 안트베르펜은 무엇일까?

    _____ , what were Antwerp?

(2) 파트라슈를 괴롭힌 것은 그가 그 곳에 들어간다는 사실이 아니었다.
    It was not the fact of his going into them which disturbe ▢

    _____ .

(3) 가난해서 돈을 낼 수 없다는 이유만으로 볼 수 없다니 너무해!
    It is so terrible not to see them ▢

    _____ !

Answer

A. (1) 그곳에 위대하고 유서 깊은 오래된 성지들이 현대의 불결함과, 분주함, 군중과 추함, 그리고 장삿속이 판치는 한가운데에 갇힌 채 남아 있다. (2) 대단한 거장의 위대함은 안트베르펜이 깃들여 있으며, 그의 영광은 우리가 어디로 향하건 그 좁은 골목 안에 존재하고 있어서, 모든 초라한 것들도 그로 인해 변했다. (3) 왜 냐하면 루벤스의 무덤이 있는 그 도시는 오직 그 한 사람을 통해 우리에게 살아있기 때문이다. (4) 그를 걱정

(4) 그런 꿈들은 듣는 사람의 공감을 불러일으키도록 말로 표현하기가 쉽지 않다.

_____ to awake

the slow sympathies of human auditors.

C. 다음 주어진 문구가 알맞은 문장이 되도록 순서를 맞춰 보세요.

(1) 파트라슈의 삶에 불안을 주는 일이 단 한 가지가 있었다.
   (which / one thing / his life / There was / caused / only / any
   uneasiness / in / Patrasche)
   →

(2) 그것들을 볼 수만 있다면, 죽어도 좋을 텐데.
   (I / would be / them, content / only / I could / If / see / to die)
   →

(3) 넬로는 미래에 작은 땅덩어리를 경작하는 것 외에 다른 일들을 꿈꾸었다.
   (other things / Nello / of / in / dreamed / than / the future.)
   → _____ of
   tillingthe little rood of earth.

(4) 그분은 언제든, 매일 우리가 그것들을 보게 해 주셨을 텐데.
   (would / He / them / have / see / us / every day / any day, / had)
   →

D. 다음 단어에 대한 맞는 설명과 연결해 보세요.

(1) bleak   ▶   ◀ ① cannot feel anything

(2) numb   ▶   ◀ ② very dirty, unpleasant conditions

(3) squalor   ▶   ◀ ③ stop doing

(4) desist   ▶   ◀ ④ cold, dull, and unpleasant

4

There was only one other / beside Patrasche / to whom
단 한 사람이 더 있었다   파트라슈 외에   넬로가 말할 수 있는

Nello could talk / at all / of his daring fantasies. This other
사람이   모든 것을 그의 대담한 꿈에 대해.

was little Alois, / who lived at the old red mill / on the
바로 알루아라는 소녀였다,   오래된 빨간 풍차 방앗간에 살았던

grassy mound, / and whose father, / the miller, / was the
푸른 잔디가 깔린 언덕 위에,   그의 아버지는,   방앗간 주인인,

best-to-do husbandman / in all the village. Little Alois
가장 부유한 농부였다   온 마을에서.

was only a pretty baby / with soft round, rosy features, /
알루아는 그저 예쁜 아이였다   매끈하게 동그랗고, 발그레한 얼굴을 가진,

made lovely / by those sweet dark eyes / that the Spanish
그리고 사랑스럽게 보였다 귀엽고 검은 눈동자로 인해   스페인의 통치가 남긴 유산인

rule has left in / so many a Flemish face, / in testimony of
수많은 플란다스 사람들의 얼굴에,

the Alvan dominion, / as Spanish art has left broadsown
알바 총독의 통치의 증거로,   스페인 미술은 널리 퍼뜨려 놓은 것과 마찬가지로

/ throughout the country / majestic palaces and stately
전국에 걸쳐   장엄한 궁전과 품위 있는 저택들,

courts, / gilded house-fronts and sculptured lintels / —
그리고 금박을 입힌 문과 조각 문틀 장식을

histories in blazonry / and poems in stone.
— 이는 장식에 담긴 역사이며   돌에 새겨진 시였다.

Little Alois was often with Nello and Patrasche. They
알루아는 자주 넬로와 파트라슈와 함께 지냈다.

played in the fields, / they ran in the snow, / they gathered
그들은 들판에서 놀았고,   눈밭에서 달렸으며,

the daisies and bilberries, / they went up to the old gray
데이지 꽃과 월엽나무 열매를 따러 다녔고,   오래된 회색 성당에 함께 올라가기도 했으며,

church together, / and they often sat together / by the broad
                    종종 함께 앉곤 했다   널찍한 아궁이 옆에

wood-fire / in the mill-house. Little Alois, / indeed, / was
            방앗간의.   알루아는,   정말로,

the richest child / in the hamlet. She had neither brother
가장 부자인 아이였다   마을에서.   형제도 자매도 없었고;

nor sister; / her blue serge dress / had never a hole in it; /
파란 모직 드레스에는   구멍이 난 적도 없었으며;

at Kermesse / she had / as many gilded nuts and *Agni Dei
명절 장에서는   갖고 있었다   금박을 입힌 견과류와 설탕 바른 아기 양 모양의 과자를

in sugar / as her hands could hold; / and when she went up
손으로 쥘 수 있는 최대한 많이;   그리고 첫 영성체를 할 때에는

for her first communion / her flaxen curls were covered /
황갈색의 곱슬머리에 썼다

with a cap of richest **Mechlin lace, / which had been her
최고급 메크린 산 레이스로 만든 미사포를,   그것은 어머니의 것이었고

mother's / and her grandmother's / before it came to her.
할머니의 것이었다   그녀가 물려받기 전에.

Men spoke already, / though she had but twelve years, / of
사람들은 벌써 말했다.   아직 12살 밖에 안 되었는데도,

the good wife she would be / for their sons to woo and win;
그녀가 좋은 아내가 될 것이라고   자신의 아들들이 청혼하여 승낙을 받아낼;

/ but she herself was / a little gay, / simple child, / in nowise
하지만 알루아 자신은   어리고 명랑하며,   천진난만한 아이일 뿐이었고,

conscious / of her heritage, / and she loved no playfellows /
관심도 없었다   물려받을 재산에,   그리고 그 어떤 친구도 좋아하지 않았다

so well as Jehan Daas's grandson and his dog.
예한 다스의 손자와 그의 개만큼.

Key Expression

neither A nor B : A도 B도 아닌
neither A nor B는 둘 다 아니라는 뜻의 상관접속사입니다.
이처럼 짝을 이뤄 쓰는 상관접속사 구문에서 A와 B 자리에는 같은 형태의 단어
나 구, 절이 와야 하는 것에 주의하세요.

ex) She had neither brother nor sister.
그녀에게는 형제도 자매도 없었다.

* 아기 양 모양의 과자(라틴어로 하나님의 어린양이라는 의미)
** 안트베르펜의 한 도시

daring 대담한 | grassy 푸른 잔디가 깔린 | miller 방앗간 주인 | husbandman 농부, 사업가 | dominion 주권,
지배 | stately 저택 | gilded 금을 입힌 | lintel 실내 창틀, 상인방 | blazonry 장식 | daisy 데이지 꽃 | bilberry
월귤나무 열매 | serge 모직 | communion 영성체 | lace 미사포 | nowise 절대로 | conscious 알고 있는 |
heritage 상속물 | playfellow 놀이 친구

One day / her father, / Baas Cogez, / a good man, / but
하루는　　　그녀의 아버지인,　코제 나리가,　　선량한 사람이지만,

somewhat stern, / came / on a pretty group / in the long
다소 엄격한 편인,　　다가왔다　놀고 있는 아이들에게　　넓은 목초지에서

meadow / behind the mill, / where the aftermath had that
풍차 뒷편의,　　　그날 두벌베기를 갓 마친 곳이었다.

day been cut. It was his little daughter / sitting amidst the
그의 어린 딸이었다　　　　　마른 풀 사이에 앉아 있는 것은,

hay, / with the great tawny head of Patrasche / on her lap,
파트라슈의 커다란 황갈색 머리를　　　무릎에 올려놓은 채,

/ and many wreaths of poppies and blue corn-flowers /
그리고 양귀비꽃과 파란 수레국화로 만든 화환 여러 개를

round them both: / on a clean smooth slab of pine wood /
둘 다 쓰고 있었으며:　　깨끗하고 매끄러운 소나무 석판 위에

the boy Nello drew their likeness / with a stick of charcoal.
넬로는 그들의 초상을 그리고 있었다　　숯 토막으로.

The miller stood / and looked at the portrait / with tears in
방앗간 주인은 서서　　초상화를 바라보았다　　두 눈에 눈물이

his eyes, / it was so strangely like, / and he loved his only
고인 채,　　그 그림은 신기하게도 닮아 있었고,　그는 외동딸을 너무나도 사랑했다.

child closely and well. Then he roughly chid the little girl
그리고는 어린 소녀를 거칠게 꾸짖고

/ for idling there / whilst her mother needed her within, /
빈둥거리고 있다며　　어머니가 집안에서 일손이 필요한데도,

and sent her indoors / crying and afraid: / then, / turning, /
그리고 딸을 집 안으로 들여보냈다　울며 무서워 하는:　그런 후,　돌아서서,

he snatched the wood / from Nello's hands. "Dost do much
판자를 낚아챘다　　넬로의 손에서.　　"이런 바보 같은 짓을

of such folly?" / he asked, / but there was a tremble / in his
할 거냐?"　　그가 물었다,　하지만 떨림이 있었다

voice.
그의 목소리에는.

Nello colored / and hung his head. "I draw everything I
넬로는 얼굴을 붉히며　고개를 숙였다.　　"저는 눈에 보이는 모든 걸 그리거든요,"

see," / he murmured.
그가 웅얼거렸다.

The miller was silent: / then he stretched his hand out / with
방앗간 주인은 말없이 있다가: 손을 내밀었다

a franc in it. "It is folly, / as I say, / and evil waste of time:
1프랑이 들어있는.   "바보 같은 짓이야, 내가 장담하는데, 사악한 시간 낭비일 뿐이야:

/ nevertheless, / it is like Alois, / and will please the house-
그렇지만,   이 그림은 알루아를 닮았고, 알루아 엄마를 기쁘게 하겠지.

mother. Take this silver bit for it / and leave it for me."
대신 이 은화를 가져가고.   그리고 그것을 내게 주렴."

somewhat 어딘지, 약간 | stern 굳은, 엄한 | aftermath 두벌베기, 일 | lap 무릎 | poppy 양귀비 | corn-flower
수레국화 | slab 널판 | likeness 초상 | charcoal 숯 | chid 혼내다 | indoor 집안에서 | snatch 낚아 채다 | dost
[고어] do you의 의미 | folly 어리석은 짓

59

The color died / out of the face of the young Ardennois; / he
핏기가 가셨다   어린 아르덴 소년의 얼굴에서;

lifted his head / and put his hands behind his back. "Keep
그는 고개를 들며   손을 등 뒤로 감췄다.

your money and the portrait both, / Baas Cogez," / he said, /
"돈과 초상화를 둘 다 가지세요,   코제 나리,"   그가 말했다,

simply. "You have been often good to me." Then / he called
순진하게.   "저한테 종종 잘해 주셨잖아요."   그리고는

Patrasche to him, / and walked away / across the field.
파트라슈를 불러,   가 버렸다   들판을 가로질러.

"I could have seen them / with that franc," / he murmured
"그 그림들을 볼 수 있었을 텐데   그 돈이 있었으면,"   파트라슈에게 속삭였다,

to Patrasche, / "but I could not sell her picture / — not even
"하지만 알루아의 그림은 팔 수 없었어   — 아무리 그 그림

for them."
들이 보고 싶어도."

Baas Cogez went into his mill-house / sore troubled in his
코제 나리는 그의 방앗간 집으로 돌아갔다   쓸쓸한 마음으로.

mind. "That lad must not beso much with Alois," / he said
"그 녀석을 알루아와 있게 해선 안 되겠어."   그가 아내에게

to his wife / that night. "Trouble may come of it / hereafter:
말했다   그 날 밤.   "무슨 문제가 생길지 몰라   앞으로:

/ he is fifteen now, / and she is twelve; / and the boy is
그 녀석은 지금 15살이고,   우리 애는 12살이고;

comely of face and form."
게다가 그 애는 제법 잘 생겼으니."

"And he is a good lad / and a loyal," / said the housewife, /
"게다가 착한 아이이고   성실해요,"   아내가 말했다,

feasting her eyes / on the piece of pine wood / where it was
즐겁게 바라보며   소나무 판자를

throned above the chimney / a cuckoo clock in oak / and a
난로 위에 위엄 있게 자리 잡은   참나무로 된 뻐꾸기 시계와

Calvary in wax.
밀랍 그리스도 십자가상과 함께.

---

hereafter 앞으로 | comely 용모가 아름다운, 고운 | cuckoo clock 뻐꾸기 시계 | Calvary 그리스도 십자가상

"Yea, / I do not gainsay that," / said the miller, / draining
"그래, 그걸 부인하는 건 아니야." 방앗간 주인이 말했다,

his pewter flagon.
백랍 포도주병을 따르며.

"Then, / if what you think of / were ever to come to pass,"
"그러면, 만일 당신이 생각하는 게 만에 하나라도 일어난다면,"

/ said the wife, / hesitatingly, / "would it matter so much?
아내가 말했다, 망설이며, "그게 그리 문제가 될까요?

She will have enough / for both, / and one cannot be better
알루아에겐 충분한 재산이 있고 두 사람이 살기에,

than happy."
그러면 그보다 더 행복할 수는 없을 텐데."

"You are a woman, / and therefore a fool," / said the
"당신은 여자야, 그래서 어리석다고." 방앗간 주인이 말했다,

miller, / harshly, / striking his pipe on the table. "The lad
거칠게, 그의 담뱃대로 식탁을 치며.

is naught but a beggar, / and, / with these painter's fancies,
"그 녀석은 거지일 뿐이야, 그리고, 이렇게 화가가 되려는 환상을 가졌으니,

/ worse than a beggar. Have a care / that they are not
거지보다 못 하다고. 신경을 쓰도록 해 그 애들이 함께 있지 못하도록

together / in the future, / or I will send the child / to the
앞으로는, 그렇지 않으면 애를 보낼 테니까

surer keeping of the nuns of the Sacred Heart."
새크리트 하트의 수녀원으로."

The poor mother was terrified, / and promised humbly to
가엾은 어머니는 겁을 먹고, 온순히 남편 뜻에 따르기로 약속했다.

do his will. Not that / she could bring herself / altogether
그렇게는 그녀 자신은 할 수 없었다 완전히

/ to separate the child / from her favorite playmate, / nor
딸을 떼어놓는 일을 제일 좋아하는 친구로부터,

did the miller even desire / that extreme of cruelty / to a
또한 방앗간 주인도 원한 것은 아니었기에 그렇게 잔인하게 대하기를

young lad / who was guilty of nothing / except poverty.
어린 아이에게 아무 잘못이 없는 가난하다는 사실 외에는.

gainsay 부인하다 | drain 비우다, 따르다 | pewter 백랍 | flagon (포도주를 담는) 큰 병 | naught 쓸모없는,
무가치의(=nothing)

But there were many ways / in which little Alois was kept
하지만 여러 방법이 있었다 / 알루아를 떨어뜨려 놓는 데에는

away / from her chosen companion; / and Nello, / being a
직접 고른 단짝으로부터; / 그리고 넬로는,

boy proud and quiet and sensitive, / was quickly wounded,
자존심 강하고 말수가 적고 예민한 소년이라서, / 바로 마음에 상처를 받았다,

/ and ceased to turn his own steps / and those of Patrasche,
그래서 발걸음을 돌리는 것을 그만두었다 / 파트라슈와 함께,

/ as he had been used to do / with every moment of leisure,
예전에 그랬던 것처럼 / 항상 틈날 때마다,

/ to the old red mill / upon the slope. What his offence was
오래된 빨간 풍차 방앗간으로 / 언덕 위의. / 그의 잘못이 무엇이었는지

/ he did not know: / he supposed / he had / in some manner
그는 알지 못했다: / 하지만 짐작했다 / 자신이 / 어떤 식으로든

/ angered Baas Cogez / by taking the portrait of Alois / in
코제 나리를 화나게 했다고 / 알루아의 초상화를 그린 것 때문에

the meadow; / and when the child who loved him / would
풀밭에서; / 그래서 사랑하는 그 애가

run to him / and nestle her hand in his, / he would smile at
뛰어와서 / 손을 잡으려 하면, / 그는 그녀에게 미소를 지으며

her / very sadly / and say / with a tender concern / for her
매우 슬프게 / 말하곤 했다 / 다정하게 걱정하며

before himself, / "Nay, Alois, / do not anger your father.
자신과 만나는 것에 대해, / "안 돼, 알루아, / 아버지를 화나게 하지 마.

He thinks that / I make you idle, dear, / and he is not
나리는 생각하시는 거야 / 내가 널 게으르게 만든다고 / 그리고 좋아하지 않으셔

pleased / that you should be with me. He is a good man /
네가 나랑 있는 것을. / 나리는 좋은 분이고

and loves you well: / we will not anger him, / Alois."
널 깊이 사랑하시니까: / 그런 분을 화나게 하지 말자, / 알루아."

But / it was with a sad heart / that he said it, / and the
하지만 / 쓰라린 마음으로 / 그는 그렇게 말한 것이었다,

earth did not look so bright / to him / as it had used to do /
그리고 세상은 그렇게 밝아 보이지 않았다 / 그에게는 / 예전에 그랬던 것처럼

cease 멈추다 | nestle 깃들이다, 자리잡다 | flaxen 담황갈색 | mill-wicket 방앗간의 쪽문 | pang 아픔 | mill-gear 방앗간 기구 | unbarred 빗장을 푼

when he went out / at sunrise / under the poplars / down the
집을 나설 때에도　　동틀 녘에　　포플러 나무 아래로

straight roads / with Patrasche. The old red mill / had been
길을 걸어 내려가도　파트라슈와 함께.　　오래된 빨간 풍차는

a landmark / to him, / and he had been used to pause / by it,
이정표와 같았고　그에게는,　　잠시 멈추곤 했었다　　그 옆에,

/ going and coming, / for a cheery greeting / with its people
오가는 길에,　　　밝게 인사를 나누기 위해　　　그 집 사람들과,

/ as her little flaxen head rose / above the low mill-wicket,
그러면 알루아는 황갈색 머리를 내밀고　　낮은 방앗간 쪽문 위로,

/ and her little rosy hands had held out / a bone or a crust /
작은 장밋빛 손을 내밀어　　　　뼈다귀나 빵조각을 건넸었다

to Patrasche. Now / the dog looked wistfully / at a closed
파트라슈에게.　하지만 이제　파트라슈는 아쉬워하며 바라보았고　　닫힌 문을,

door, / and the boy went on / without pausing, / with a pang
소년은 계속 걸어갔다　　　멈추지 않고,　　　아픔을 느끼며

/ at his heart, / and the child sat within / with tears dropping
마음속에,　　그리고 알루아는 집 안에 앉아 있었다　눈물을 뚝뚝 흘리며

slowly / on the knitting / to which she was set / on her little
뜨개질감 위로　　　앉아서　　　작은 의자 위에

stool / by the stove; / and Baas Cogez, / working among his
난로 옆에 있는;　코제 나리는,　　곡식 자루와 방앗간 기구 사이에

sacks and his mill-gear, / would harden his will / and say to
서 일하면서,　　　　자신의 의지를 굳히며　　스스로에게 말하

himself, / "It is best so. The lad is all but a beggar, / and full
곤 했다,　　"이것이 최선이야.　그 아이는 거지일 뿐이고,　　게으른데다,

of idle, / dreaming fooleries. Who knows / what mischief /
환상에 빠져 있으니.　　　누가 알겠어　어떤 나쁜 일이

might not come of it / in the future?" So he was wise / in his
생기게 될지　　　　　나중에?"　　　그렇게 그는 똑똑했기 때문에

generation, / and would not have the door unbarred, / except
나이에 비해,　　문의 빗장을 풀려 하지 않았다,

upon rare and formal occasion, / which seemed to have /
아주 드물게 공식적인 일이 있을 때를 제외하고,　　그리고 그런 행동은 보였다

neither warmth nor mirth in them / to the two children,
따뜻함도 즐거움도 없는 것처럼　　　　그 두 아이들에게는,

/ who had been accustomed so long / to a daily gleeful,
그들은 오랫동안 익숙했기 때문에   하루하루 즐겁고,

/ careless, / happy interchange of greeting, / speech, /
근심 없이,   행복하게 인사를 나누고,   얘기하며,

and pastime, / with no other / watcher of their sports / or
함께 지내는 것에,   다른 누구도 없이도   그들의 노는 모습을 보는 사람이나

auditor of their fancies / than Patrasche, / sagely shaking /
자신들의 공상을 들어주는 사람이   파트라슈 외에는,   지혜롭게 흔들어 주고

the brazen bells of his collar / and responding / with all a
목에 달린 놋쇠 방울을   대답해 주던   재빠르게

dog's swift sympathies / to their every change of mood.
재빠르게 기분을 맞춰주며   아이들의 모든 감정 변화에.

All this while / the little panel of pine wood remained /
이러는 동안 내내   작은 소나무 판자는 놓여 있었다

over the chimney in the mill-kitchen / with the cuckoo
방앗간 주방의 난로 위에   뻐꾸기 시계와

clock / and the waxen Calvary, / and sometimes / it seemed
밀랍 그리스도 십자가상과 함께,   그리고 가끔

to Nello a little hard / that whilst his gift was accepted / he
넬로는 조금 힘들어 보였다   자신의 선물은 받아들여졌지만

himself should be denied.
그 자신은 거부되었다는 사실에.

Key Expression ❗

the + 형용사 = 형용사 + people

the+형용사는 복수보통명사로 '~한 사람들', 즉 형용사 + people의 의미가 됩니다. 복수보통명사이므로 복수 취급을 한다는 점도 함께 기억하세요.
한편 the beautiful=beauty, the true=truth와 같이 추상명사로 사용되는 경우도 있으며 이럴 때는 단수 취급을 합니다.

ex) We are poor: we must take what God sends — the ill with the good: the poor cannot choose.
                                          (=the illness)(=the goodness)(=poor people)

우리는 가난하지: 하지만 우리는 신이 보내주신 것을 받아들여야 한다 — 나쁜 것이든 좋은 것이든: 가난한 사람들은 선택할 수 없단다.

---

sagely 지혜롭게 | brazen 놋쇠 | reverent 공경하는 | vague 막연한, 희미한 | beguile 매료시키다, 현혹시키다 | nay 아니다 (no의 옛글투) | cornfield 옥수수밭 | piteously 불쌍하게, 측은하게 | morrow 내일, 다음 날 (=tomorrow) | saint's day 영명축일, 세례명을 기념하는 날 | barn 헛간

But he did not complain: / it was his habit / to be quiet: /
하지만 그는 불평하지 않았다:　　　　그의 습관이었다　　　조용히 있는 것은:

old Jehan Daas had said ever / to him, / "We are poor: / we
예한 다스 할아버지는 말한 적이 있다　　　그에게,　　　"우리는 가난하단다:

must take / what God sends — / the ill with the good: / the
받아들여야 하지　신이 보내주신 것을 —　　　좋은 일도 나쁜 일도:

poor cannot choose."
가난한 사람들은 선택할 수 없단다."

To which / the boy had always listened / in silence, / being
그런 말을　　　소년은 항상 귀 기울여 들었다　　　잠자코,

reverent / of his old grandfather; / but nevertheless / a
공경했기 때문에　나이 많으신 할아버지를;　　　하지만 그럼에도 불구하고

certain vague, sweet hope, / such as beguiles the children
어떤 막연하고, 달콤한 희망이,　　　천재성을 가진 아이들이 가지는 것과 같은,

of genius, / had whispered / in his heart, / "Yet / the poor
　　　속삭였다　　　그의 마음속에서,　　"하지만　가난한 사람들도

do choose / sometimes — / choose to be great, / so that
선택할 수 있어　때로는 —　　　위대한 사람이 되는 거야,

men cannot say them nay." / And he thought so still / in
사람들이 함부로 대하지 못하도록."　　　그래서 그는 아직 그렇게 생각했다

his innocence; / and one day, / when the little Alois, /
순진한 마음에;　　　그리고 어느 날,　　　알루아가,

finding him / by chance / alone / among the cornfields / by
그를 발견하고　우연히　　홀로 있는 것을　옥수수 밭에

the canal, / ran to him / and held him close, / and sobbed
운하 옆,　　그에게 달려가　　그를 꼭 안고,　　　가엾게 흐느끼자

piteously / because the morrow / would be her saint's day,
　　　왜냐하면 그 이튿날이　　　그녀의 영명축일이었고,

/ and for the first time in all her life / her parents had failed
생전 처음으로　　　　　　　그녀의 부모님이 그를 초대하지 않았

to bid him / to the little supper / and romp / in the great
기 때문에　　작은 잔치를 열고　　　뛰어노는 자리에　넓은 헛간에서

barns / with which her feast-day was always celebrated,
　　　그녀의 축일을 항상 축하해 줬던,

/ Nello had kissed her / and murmured to her / in firm
넬로는 알루아에게 입을 맞추며   속삭였다   확고한 믿음을

faith, / "It shall be different / one day, / Alois. One day /
갖고,   "달라질 거야   언젠가는,   알루아.   언젠가는

that little bit of pine wood / that your father has of mine /
내 작은 소나무 판이   너희 아버지가 갖고 계신

shall be worth / its weight in silver; / and he will not shut
가치가 있을 거야   그 무게의 은덩이만큼의;   그러면 그분도 문을 닫아 버리진

the door / against me / then. Only love me / always, / dear
않으실 거야   내 앞에서   그때에는. 그저 나를 사랑해 줘 언제까지나,

little Alois, / only love me always, / and I will be great."
사랑하는 알루아,   그저 언제까지나 사랑해 줘,   그러면 나는 위대한 사람이 될 거야."

"And / if I do not love you?" / the pretty child asked, /
"그런데   만약 내가 널 사랑하지 않으면?"   귀여운 아이가 물었다,

pouting a little through her tears, / and moved by the
눈물 사이로 입을 삐죽 내밀며,   그리고 본능적인 애교 섞인

instinctive / coquetries of her sex.
행동을 하며   여자 아이 특유의.

Nello's eyes left her face / and wandered to the distance,
넬로의 시선은 그녀의 얼굴에서 벗어나   먼 곳을 바라보았다,

/ where / in the red and gold of the Flemish night / the
    그곳에는   플란다스의 붉은색과 황금색의 밤하늘에

cathedral spire rose. There was a smile on his face / so
성당의 뾰족탑이 우뚝 솟아 있었다. 그의 얼굴에는 미소가 번졌다   너무나 감미

sweet and yet so sad / that little Alois was awed by it. "I
로우면서도 한편으론 슬픔에 젖은   알루아가 감탄할 정도로.

will be great still," / he said / under his breath — / "great
"그래도 나는 위대한 사람이 될 거야," 그는 말했다 나지막한 소리로—   "위대한 사람이,

still, / or die, / Alois."
아니면 죽고 말 거야, 알루아."

"You do not love me," / said the little spoilt child, /
"너는 날 사랑하지 않는구나," 응석받이 소녀가 말했다,

---

* 성가족 그림- 어린 예수와 성모마리아와 요셉을 그린 그림

pout 입을 삐죽 내밀다 | instinctive 본능적인 | coquetry 애교, 아양부리기 | spoilt 응석부리는, 버릇없는 |
throng 모이다 | grandsire 할아버지 | luxuriant 호화스러운, 화려한 | slope 언덕outward: 바깥을 향한

pushing him away; / but the boy shook his head / and
그를 밀쳐내며;   하지만 소년은 고개를 저으며   웃어 보였다,

smiled, / and went on his way / through the tall yellow
그리고 가던 길을 걸어가며   키 큰 노란 옥수수 밭을 헤치며,

corn, / seeing as in a vision / some day in a fair future /
환상 속에서 떠올려 보았다   아름다운 미래의 어느 날을

when he should come into that old familiar land / and ask
그가 그 오래된 낯익은 땅에 돌아와서   알루아에게

Alois of her people, / and be not refused or denied, / but
가족에 대해 물었을 때,   거절당하거나 외면당하지 않고,   대신

received in honor, / whilst the village folk should throng /
정중한 대우를 받는 장면을,   그리고 마을 사람들이 몰려들어

to look upon him / and say in one another's ears, / "Dost
그를 보려고   서로의 귀에다 속삭이는 모습을,   "그가 보여?

see him? He is a king among men, / for he is a great artist
그는 사람들 중의 황이야,   위대한 화가가 되었고

/ and the world speaks his name; / and yet he was only
세상이 그를 칭송하니까;   하지만 그는 그저 우리의 가엾은

our poor little Nello, / who was a beggar as one may say,
넬로였을 뿐인데,   거의 거지나 다름없었고,

/ and only got his bread / by the help of his dog." And he
겨우 끼니를 때웠는데   개의 도움으로."   그는 또 생각

thought / how he would fold his grandsire / in furs and
했다   그의 할아버지에게는 입혀 드리고   모피로 된 보랏빛 옷을,

purples, / and portray him / as the old man is portrayed in
그려 드리는 모습을   성가족 그림 속 노인의 모습과 같이

*the Family / in the chapel of St. Jacques; / and of how he
성 쟈크 성당에 있는;   그리고 파트라슈의 목에

would hang the throat of Patrasche / with a collar of gold,
매어 주고   금 목걸이를,

/ and place him on his right hand, / and say to the people,
자신의 오른편에 앉힌 후,   사람들에게 말하는 모습을,

/ "This was once my only friend;" / and of how he would
"이 개가 예전에 제 유일한 친구였어요;"   그리고 직접 짓고

build himself / a great white marble palace, / and make
거대한 흰 대리석 궁전을,   자신에게 만들어 주는

to himself / luxuriant gardens of pleasure, / on the slope /
모습을   화려한 기쁨의 정원을,   언덕 위에   67

looking outward / to where the cathedral spire rose, / and
바라다 보이는　　　　성모 대성당의 뾰족탑이 솟아오른 곳이,

not dwell in it himself, / but summon to it, / as to a home,
그리고 자신은 그 안에 살지 않고,　대신 그 집을 부르는 모습을,　집이라고,

/ all men young and poor and friendless, / but of the will
모든 어리고 가난하고 친구도 없는 아이들을 위한,　　　　하지만 뜻을 간직한

/ to do mighty things; / and of how he would say to them
위대한 일을 하겠다는;　　그리고 그들에게 항상 말하는 모습을,

always, / if they sought to bless his name, / "Nay, do not
　　　그들이 그의 이름을 축복하려 하면,　　　　"아니에요, 제게 감사하지

thank me / — thank Rubens. Without him, / what should I
마세요　　— 루벤스 님께 감사하세요. 그분이 없었다면,　제가 무엇이 되었겠어요?"

have been?" And these dreams, / beautiful, / impossible, /
　　　　그리고 이러한 꿈들이,　아름답고,　불가능하지만,

innocent, / free of all selfishness, / full of heroical worship,
순수하고,　아무런 이기심도 없으며,　거장에 대한 존경심으로 가득한,

/ were so closely about him / as he went / that he was happy
　그의 곁에 있었기에　　　　그는 걸어가면서　행복했다

/ — happy / even on this sad anniversary / of Alois's saint's
　— 행복해 했다　이런 슬픈 기념일에도　　알루아의 영명축일인,

day, / when he and Patrasche went home / by themselves /
그와 파트라슈가 집으로 가서　　　　단둘이

to the little dark hut / and the meal of black bread, / whilst
작고 어두운 오두막에서　　검은 빵으로 끼니를 때울 때,

in the mill-house / all the children of the village / sang and
한편 방앗간 집에서는　　온 마을의 아이들이 모여　　　노래하고 웃으며

laughed, / and ate the big round cakes of *Dijon / and the
　　　　크고 둥그런 디종 케이크와　　　　브라반트 아몬드

almond gingerbread of Brabant, / and danced / in the great
생강빵을 먹고,　　　　　춤을 추었다　넓은 헛간에서

barn / to the light of the stars / and the music of flute and
　별빛에 맞추어　　　또한 플루트와 바이올린 음악에 맞추어.

fiddle.

"Never mind, Patrasche," / he said, / with his arms round
"괜찮아, 파트라슈,"　　　그가 말했다,　팔로 파트라슈의 목을 끌어안고

the dog's neck / as they both sat / in the door of the hut, /
함께 앉아서   오두막의 문간에,

where / the sounds of the mirth / at the mill / came down
그곳에서는   잔치 소리가   방앗간의   들려왔다

to them / on the night air / — "never mind. It shall all be
밤공기를 타고   — "괜찮아.   모든 것이 달라질 거야

changed / by and by."
조금씩."

He believed in the future: / Patrasche, / of more experience
넬로는 미래를 믿었다: 하지만 파트라슈는, 경험도 더 풍부하고

/ and of more philosophy, / thought / that the loss of the
생각도 더 깊었기에,   생각했다   방앗간 집 잔치에 초대받지 못한 슬픔이

mill supper / in the present / was ill compensated / by
지금   가려진 것뿐이라고

dreams / of milk and honey / in some vague hereafter. And
그의 꿈에 의해 젖과 꿀이 흐르는   어느 어렴풋한 미래의.

Patrasche growled / whenever he passed / by Baas Cogez.
그래서 파트라슈는 으르렁댔다   지나갈 때마다   코제 씨의 곁을.

"This is Alois's name-day, / is it not?" / said the old man
"오늘은 알루아의 영명축일이지,   그렇지 않니?"   다스 할아버지가 말했다

Daas / that night / from the corner / where he was stretched
그날 밤   방구석에서   그가 누워 있던

/ upon his bed of sacking.
마른 짚으로 된 침대 위에.

The boy gave a gesture of assent: / he wished / that the old
소년은 그렇다는 몸짓을 취해 보였다: 그리고 그는 바랐다

man's memory had erred a little, / instead of keeping such
할아버지의 기억력이 조금은 나빠졌기를,   그렇게 정확하게 기억하지 못하고.

sure account.

---

* 파리에서 남동쪽에 있는 디종은 1179년부터 1477년까지 부르고뉴공국의 수도였으며, 지금도 중세의 저택과 교회가 많이 남아 있음

outward 밖으로 향하는 | dwell 살다, 거주하다 | summon 불러모으다 | friendless 친구가 없는 | heroical 영웅에 대한 | anniversary 기념일 | gingerbread 생강빵 | fiddle 바이올린 | mirth 유쾌, 기쁨 | by and by 차츰 차츰 | philosophy 생각 | compensate 상쇄하다, 보상하다 | milk and honey 젖과 꿀(풍요로움의 상징) | name-day 영명축일(=saint's day) | sacking 거친 삼베, 지프라기 | assent 동의

"And / why not there?" / his grandfather pursued. "Thou
"그럼   왜 거기 가지 않았니?"   할아버지가 물었다.

hast never missed a year / before, / Nello."
"한 번도 빠진 적이 없었잖니   전에는,   넬로."

"Thou art too sick / to leave," / murmured the lad, /
"할아버지가 편찮으셔서   두고 갈 수 없어요,"   소년이 중얼거렸다.

bending his handsome head / over the bed.
잘생긴 얼굴을 숙이며   침대 위로.

"Tut! Tut! Mother Nulette would have come / and sat
"쯧!   쯧!   눌레트 부인이 와서   있어 주었을 텐데.

with me, / as she does scores of times. What is the cause,
매번 그랬잖니.   이유가 무엇이냐,

Nello?" / the old man persisted. "Thou surely hast not had
넬로?"   할아버지가 다그쳤다.   "설마 다툰 것은 아니겠지

ill words / with the little one?"
그 아이랑?"

"Nay, / grandfather / — never," / said the boy quickly, /
"아니에요,   할아버지   — 절대 아니에요," 소년은 얼른 대답했다.

with a hot color / in his bent face. "Simply and truly, / Baas
화끈 달아올라   숙인 얼굴이.   "사실을 말하자면,

Cogez did not have me asked / this year. He has taken some
코제 나리가 부르지 않으셨어요   올해.   제게 마음이 상하셨거든요"

whim against me."

"But thou hast done nothing wrong?"
"네가 무슨 잘못을 했기에?"

"That I know / — nothing. I took the portrait of Alois / on
"그건 저도   — 모르겠어요.   저는 알루아의 초상화를 그린 것뿐이에요

a piece of pine: / that is all."
소나무 판에: 그게 전부인 걸요."

"Ah!" The old man was silent: / the truth suggested itself to
"아!"   할아버지는 말이 없었다: 진실이 밝혀졌기 때문에

him / with the boy's innocent answer. He was tied / to a bed
소년의 솔직한 대답으로 인해.   그는 꼼짝 못 했지만

of dried leaves in the corner / of a wattle hut, / but he had
마른 잎으로 만든 침대 구석에서   나뭇가지를 엮어 지은 오두막의,

not wholly forgotten / what the ways of the world were like.
완전히 잊어버린 것은 아니었다   세상이 돌아가는 이치가 어떠한지를.

He drew Nello's fair head fondly / to his breast / with a
그는 넬로의 고운 얼굴을 다정하게 안았다   그의 가슴에

tenderer gesture. "Thou art very poor, my child," / he said /
다정한 몸짓으로.   "너는 매우 가난하단다, 아가야."   그는 말했다

with a quiver the more / in his aged, / trembling voice — /
더욱 떨면서   여느 노인보다   떨리는 목소리로 —

"so poor! It is very hard for thee."
"너무나 가난하지! 네게는 너무 힘들 거야."

"Nay, / I am rich," / murmured Nello; / and in his innocence
"아니에요, 전 부자예요."   넬로가 나지막하게 말했다;   그리고 순진한 마음에

/ he thought so / — rich / with the imperishable powers / that
그는 그렇게 생각했다   — 부자라고   불멸의 능력을 가진

are mightier / than the might of kings.
더욱 위대한   왕이 가진 권위보다.

And he went / and stood / by the door of the hut / in the quiet
그리고 그는 걸어가서   서 있었다   오두막의 문 곁에

autumn night, / and watched / the stars troop by / and the tall
조용한 가을 밤에,   그리고 바라보았다   별들이 무리지어 빛나는 모습을   그리고 키 큰

poplars / bend and shiver / in the wind. All the casements /
포플러 나무가 휘어지거나 떨리는 모습을   바람에.   모든 창에는

of the mill-house / were lighted, / and every now and then /
방앗간 집의   불이 밝혀져 있었다,   그리고 때때로

the notes of the flute came to him. The tears fell down / his
플루트 소리가 그에게 들려왔다.   눈물이 흘러내렸다   그의

cheeks, / for he was but a child, / yet he smiled, / for he said
볼을 타고,   그는 그저 어린애였기 때문에,   하지만 미소지었다,   혼잣말을 하면서,

to himself, / "In the future!" He stayed there / until all was
"두고 봐!"   그는 그곳에 서 있었다

quite still and dark, / then he and Patrasche / went within /
모든 것이 조용하고 캄캄할 때까지,   그러고는 그와 파트라슈는   집 안으로 들어가

and slept together, / long and deeply, / side by side.
함께 잠들었다,   길고 깊게,   나란히 누워서.

---

fondly 애정을 담아 | thee 너를, 너에게(=목적격 you의 고어) | imperishable 불멸의 | troop 무리, 무리지어 가다
| casement 창 | note 음, 소리 | side by side 나란히

71

mini test 4

A. 다음 문장을 해석해 보세요.

(1) Men spoke already, / though she had but twelve years, / of the good wife she would be / for their sons to woo and win.
→

(2) If what you think of / were ever to come to pass, / would it matter so much?
→

(3) It seemed to Nello a little hard / that whilst his gift was accepted / he himself should be denied.
→

(4) One day / that little bit of pine wood / that your father has of mine / shall be worth / its weight in silver.
→

B. 다음 주어진 문구가 알맞은 문장이 되도록 순서를 맞춰 보세요.

(1) 그것 대신에 이 은화를 가져가고 그걸 내게 주렴.
[this / leave / Take / for / for / it / silver bit / and / it / me]
→

(2) 그 돈이 있었으면 그 그림들을 볼 수 있었을 텐데.
[have / I / seen / them / could / that franc / with]
→

(3) 미래에 어떤 나쁜 일이 생기지 않을지 누가 알겠어?
[mischief / what / in / might not / it / the future / come of]
Who knows ⬚⬚⬚⬚⬚⬚⬚⬚⬚⬚⬚⬚⬚⬚⬚⬚⬚⬚⬚ ?

(4) 그는 세상이 돌아가는 이치가 어떠한지를 완전히 잊어버린 것은 아니었다.
[like / the ways / the world / of / were / what]
He had not wholly forgotten _____

_____ .

C. 다음 주어진 문장이 본문의 내용과 맞으면 T, 틀리면 F에 동그라미 하세요.

(1) Alois was the only child in her family.
[T / F]

(2) Alois' father allow her to play with Nello.
[T / F]

(3) Nello deamed of being a great artist.
[T / F]

(4) Nello's grandfather couldn't understand why Nello didn't go to alois.
[T / F]

D. 의미가 비슷한 것끼리 서로 연결해 보세요.

(1) perplexed   ▶   ◀ ① deny
(2) heritage   ▶   ◀ ② confused
(3) gainsay   ▶   ◀ ③ attract
(4) beguile   ▶   ◀ ④ inheritance

보였다. (4) 언젠가는 너희 아버지가 가지고 계신 내 작은 소나무 판이 그 무게의 은덩이만큼의 가치를 갖게 될 거야. | B. (1) Take this silver bit for it and leave it for me. (2) I could have seen them with that franc. (3) what mischief might not come of it in the future (4) what the ways of the world were like | C. (1) T (2) F (3) T (4) F | D. (1) ② (2) ④ (3) ① (4) ③

5

Now / he had a secret / which only Patrasche knew. There
이제   넬로에게는 비밀이 생겼다   파트라슈만 알고 있는.

was a little out-house to the hut, / which no one entered /
오두막에는 작은 헛간이 있었는데,   아무도 출입하지 않는

but himself / — a dreary place, / but with abundant clear
넬로 외에는   — 초라한 곳으로서,   하지만 청명한 빛이 듬뿍 들어오는

light / from the north. Here / he had fashioned himself
북쪽으로부터.   여기에서   그는 서툴게 만들었고,

rudely, / an easel in rough lumber, / and here on a great
거친 통나무로 된 이젤을,   여기 위대한 회색 바다에

gray sea / of stretched paper / he had given shape / to one
펼쳐 놓은 종이의   그려 놓았다   수없이 많은

of the innumerable fancies / which possessed his brain. No
환상 가운데 하나를   그의 머리 속을 사로잡은.

one had ever taught him / anything; / colors / he had no
아무도 그에게 가르쳐 준 적 없었고   아무것도;   물감도   살 방법이 없었다;

means to buy; / he had gone without bread / many a time
    굶은 적도 있었다   여러 번

/ to procure even the few rude vehicles / that he had here;
몇 안 되는 조잡한 도구들을 마련하기 위해   여기 있는;

/ and it was only in black or white / that he could fashion
단지 검은색이나 흰색 뿐이었다   그가 표현할 수 있는 방법은

the things / he saw. This great figure / which he had drawn
자신이 본 것을. 이 굉장한 그림은   그가 여기에 그려 놓은

here / in chalk / was only an old man / sitting on a fallen
    석필로   노인이었다   쓰러진 나무에 걸터앉은

tree / — only that.
    — 그것 뿐이었다.

He had seen / old Michel the woodman / sitting so / at
그는 본 적이 있었다   나무꾼 마이클 할아버지가   그렇게 앉아 있는 것을

---

out-house 옥외 헛간 | rudely 서툴게 | stretched 펼쳐진 | innumerable 수없이 많은 | possess 사로잡다
| procure 마련하다 | perspective 원근법 | anatomy 해부학, 인체 | worn-out 노쇠한 | rugged 모난 |
careworn 고생에 찌든 | mournful 애처로운

evening / many a time. He had never had a soul to tell him
저녁 때면   여러 번.   어느 누구도 그에게 얘기해 준 적이 없었다

/ of outline or perspective, / of anatomy or of shadow, / and
선이나 원근법에 대해,   인체나 명암에 대해,

yet he had given / all the weary, worn-out age, / all the sad,
그렇지만 그는 표현했다   모든 피로하고, 노쇠한 나이를,   온갖 슬프고, 조용

quiet patience, / all the rugged, careworn pathos / of his
한 인내심을,   모나고, 고생에 찌든 모든 비애감을

original, / and given them / so that the old lonely figure was
그 인물의,   그리고 그 모습에 부여하여   늙고 외로운 인물은 한 편의 시가 되었다.

a poem, / sitting there, / meditative and alone, / on the dead
그곳에 앉아 있는,   명상에 잠긴 채 홀로,   죽은 나무 위에.

tree, / with the darkness / of the descending night behind
어둠을 배경으로   인물의 뒤 편에 깔려 있는 밤의.

him.

It was rude, / of course, / in a way, / and had many faults, /
그 그림은 서툴렀고, 물론,   한편으론,   결점도 많았다.

no doubt; / and yet it was real, / true in nature, / true in art,
틀림없이;   그럼에도 사실적이었고,   본질에 충실했고,   진짜 예술이었다.

/ and very mournful, / and in a manner beautiful.
그리고 매우 애처로웠으며,   또한 아름다웠다.

Patrasche had lain quiet / countless hours / watching its
파트라슈는 조용히 엎드려 있었다   수많은 시간 동안   서서히 그림이 완성되는

gradual creation / after the labor of each day was done,
것을 지켜보며   날마다 일과를 마치고 난 후,

/ and he knew / that Nello had a hope / — vain and wild
그리고 알았다   넬로에게 꿈이 있다는 것을   — 덧없고 무모할지 모르지만,

perhaps, / but strongly cherished / — of sending this
매우 소중하게 간직한   — 이 멋진 그림을 출품하겠다는 꿈을

great drawing / to compete / for a prize of two hundred
대회에   200프랑의 상금이 걸린

francs / a year / which it was announced / in Antwerp
매년   그 대회는 공지되었다   안트베르펜에서

/ would be open to every lad / of talent, / scholar or
모든 청소년이 참여할 수 있다고   재능을 가진,   학자이든 농부이든,

peasant, / under eighteen, / who would attempt to win it /
18세 이하라면,   그는 대회에서 이기고자 했다

with some unaided work / of chalk or pencil. Three of the
아무 도움 없이 완성한 작품으로   석필이나 연필로 그린.   가장 뛰어난 세 명의

foremost artists / in the town of Rubens / were to be the
화가들이   루벤스의 고장에서   심사위원이 되어

judges / and elect the victor / according to his merits.
우승자를 선정할 예정이었다   능력에 따라.

Key Expression

be to 부정사 용법

be to 부정사는 to 부정사의 특수한 형태로, 다음과 같이 다양한 의미를 지니고
있어 문맥에 따라 해석해야 합니다.

▶예정 : ~할 예정이다(=will) → 미래를 나타내는 부사/부사구와 함께
▶의무 : ~해야 한다(=should)
▶가능 : ~할 수 있다(=can) → 주로 수동태로 쓰임
▶운명 : ~할 운명이다(=be destined to)
▶의도 : ~하고자 한다(=intend to)
▶가정 : ~한다면 → 가정법에서 절대 불가능한 가정을 표현할 때

ex) The drawings were to go in on the first day of December, and the decision
(were to) be given on the twenty-fourth, so that he who should win might
rejoice with all his people at the Christmas season.
그림들은 12월 1일에 제출해야 했고, 결정은 24일에 내려질 예정이었다.
(첫 번째 were to는 예정으로 볼 수도 있으나 제출의 의무로 보는 것이, 두 번째
생략된 were to는 예정으로 해석하는 것이 자연스러워요.)

All the spring and summer and autumn / Nello had been
봄, 여름, 가을 내내 | 넬로는 작업을 계속했다

at work / upon this treasure, / which, / if triumphant, /
이 보물에 대해, | 그 작품이, | 만일 성공한다면,

would build him / his first step / toward independence and
그에게 마련해 줄 것이었다 | 첫 번째 단계를 | 독립과 예술의 신비를 향한

the mysteries of the art / which he blindly, / ignorantly, /
그가 맹목적으로, | 아무것도 모른 채,

and yet passionately adored.
하지만 열정적으로 동경했던.

He said nothing / to any one: / his grandfather would not
그는 아무 말도 하지 않았다 | 아무에게도: | 그의 할아버지는 이해하지 못했을 테니까,

have understood, / and little Alois was lost / to him. Only
그리고 알루아는 없었다 | 그의 곁에.

to Patrasche / he told all, / and whispered, / "Rubens
오직 파트라슈에게만 | 모든 것을 이야기하며, | 속삭였다.

would give it me, / I think, / if he knew."
"루벤스 님은 내게 상을 줄 거야, 그렇게 생각해, 만일 그가 알고 계시다면."

Patrasche thought so too, / for he knew / that Rubens had
파트라슈도 그렇게 생각했다. | 알았기 때문에 | 루벤스가 개를 사랑했다는

loved dogs / or he had never painted them / with such
것을 | 그렇지 않았더라면 개를 그리지 않았을 테니까

exquisite fidelity; / and men who loved dogs were, / as
그렇게 정교하게 공을 들여서; | 그리고 개를 사랑하는 사람들은,

Patrasche knew, / always pitiful.
파트라슈가 알기에, | 항상 인정이 많았으니까.

The drawings were to go in / on the first day of December,
그림들은 제출해야 했다 | 12월 1일에,

/ and the decision be given / on the twenty-fourth, / so that
그리고 결과는 발표될 예정되었다 | 24일에,

he who should win / might rejoice / with all his people / at
그래서 우승하는 사람이 | 기뻐할 수 있도록 | 그의 모든 가족들과 함께

the Christmas season.
성탄절에.

gradual 점진적인 | vain 헛된 | cherish 간직하다, 소중히 하다 | unaided 독립적으로, 혼자 힘으로 | foremost
최고의, 가장 뛰어난 | elect 선정하다 | blindly 맹목적으로 무턱대고 | exquisite 섬세한 | fidelity 충실함, 정확도
| pitiful 정이 많은

In the twilight / of a bitter wintry day, / and with a beating
황혼녘에　　어느 매섭게 추웠던 겨울날의,　　두근거리는 가슴을 안고,

heart, / with hope, / now faint with fear, / Nello placed the
희망에 들떠,　두려움으로 현기증이 날 듯이,　넬로는 그 멋진 그림을 싣고

great picture / on his little green milk-cart, / and took it, /
자신의 작은 초록색 우유 수레에,　　가져갔다,

with the help of Patrasche, / into the town, / and there left
파트라슈의 도움을 받아,　　　마을로,　　그리고 그곳에 두었다,

it, / as enjoined, / at the doors of a public building.
정해진 대로,　공회당 문 앞에.

"Perhaps / it is worth nothing at all. How can I tell?" /
"어쩌면　내 그림은 아무 가치도 없을지 몰라.　내가 어떻게 알겠어?"

he thought, / with the heart-sickness of a great timidity.
그는 생각했다,　너무 쑥스러워 울렁거림을 느끼며.

Now that he had left it there, / it seemed to him / so
왜냐하면 그림을 그곳에 두고 왔고,　그에게는 보였기 때문에

hazardous, so vain, so foolish, / to dream / that he, a
너무도 위험하고, 헛되고, 어리석은 일처럼,　꿈을 꾸는 것이

little lad with bare feet, / who barely knew his letters, /
가난뱅이인 어린 소년이,　글도 거의 모르는,

could do anything / at which great painters, / real artists,
작품을 만들 수 있기를　위대한 화가들,　진짜 예술가들이,

/ could ever deign to look. Yet he took heart / as he went
보고 싶어 하는.　하지만 그는 용기를 얻었다

by the cathedral: / the lordly form of Rubens / seemed to
대성당을 지나면서:　루벤스의 위풍당당한 풍채가　보이는 듯 했고

rise / from the fog and the darkness, / and to loom / in its
안개와 어둠 속에서,　어렴풋이 나타나　위엄 있는

magnificence / before him, / whilst the lips, / with their
모습으로　넬로의 앞에,　그 입술이,

kindly smile, / seemed to him to murmur, / "Nay, / have
인자하게 미소 지으며,　그에게 속삭이는 듯 했다,　"아니란다,

courage! It was not by a weak heart and by faint fears /
용기를 가지렴! 약한 마음과 막연한 두려움 때문이 아니었단다

that I wrote my name / for all time / upon Antwerp."
내 이름을 새겨 넣을 수 있었던 것은　언제까지나　안트베르펜 사람들에게."

faint 쓰러지다, 현기증이 나다 | enjoin 명령하다, 정하다 | heart-sickness 울렁거림 | hazardous 위험한, 모험적인
deign to (황송하게도) ~~하다 | loom 어렴풋이 나타나다

Nello ran home / through the cold night, / comforted. He
넬로는 집으로 뛰어갔다   차가운 밤 공기를 헤치며,   위안을 얻고.

had done his best: / the rest must be as God willed, / he
그는 최선을 다했고: 나머지는 하나님의 뜻하신 대로 이루어지는 것이라고,

thought, / in that innocent, unquestioning faith / which
그는 생각했다, 그런 순진하고, 의심 없는 믿음으로

had been taught him / in the little gray chapel / among the
배웠던   작은 회색 성당에서

willows and the poplar-trees.
버드 나무와 포플러 나무에 둘러 쌓인.

The winter was very sharp already. That night, / after they
그 해 겨울은 이미 혹독했다.   그 날 밤,   넬로와 파트라슈

reached the hut, / snow fell; / and fell for very many days
가 오두막에 도착한 후,   눈이 내렸다;   그리고 그 뒤로 오랫동안 계속 내렸다,

after that, / so that the paths and the divisions in the fields
그렇게 해서 들판과 밭둑의 길이,

/ were all obliterated, / and all the smaller streams were
모두 지워져 버렸고,   모든 작은 냇물들도 얼어 버렸고,

frozen over, / and the cold was intense / upon the plains.
추운 바람이 심하게 불어왔다   들판 위로.

Then, / indeed, / it became hard work / to go round for the
그래서,   정말로,   일이 너무 힘들어졌다   우유를 모으러 돌아다니고

milk / while the world was all dark, / and carry it / through
세상이 모두 어두운 동안,   실어 나르는 것은

the darkness / to the silent town. Hard work, / especially
어둠을 뚫고   쥐죽은듯 조용한 마을로. 힘은 일이었다,

for Patrasche, / for the passage of the years, / that were
특히 파트라슈에게는,   왜냐하면 지나간 몇 년의 세월이,

only bringing Nello / a stronger youth, / were bringing
넬로에게는 갖다 주었지만   건장한 젊음을,   파트라슈에게는 갖다 주었기

him / old age, / and his joints were stiff / and his bones
때문에   노쇠한 나이만을,   그래서 파트라슈의 관절은 뻣뻣해졌고   뼈는 자주 아팠다.

ached often. But he would never give up / his share of the
하지만 파트라슈는 절대 포기하지 않았다   자기 몫의 일을.

labor. Nello would fain have spared him / and drawn the
넬로가 기꺼이 그를 쉬게 하고   수레를 그가 직접 끌려고

cart himself, / but Patrasche would not allow it. All he
했지만,   파트라슈는 허락하려 하지 않았다.

would ever permit or accept / was the help / of a thrust
그가 허락하고 받아들인 것은   도움을 받는 것 뿐이었다

from behind to the truck / as it lumbered along / through
뒤에서 트럭을 밀어주는   트럭이 덜커덩거리며 넘어갈 때   언 땅에 난 바퀴

the ice-ruts. Patrasche had lived in harness, / and he was
자국을.   파트라슈는 목줄을 맨 채 살아왔고   그것을 자랑스럽게

proud of it. He suffered a great deal / sometimes / from
생각했다.   파트라슈는 무척 괴로워했다   때로는

frost, and the terrible roads, / and the rheumatic pains of
서릿발과, 험악한 길과,   류머티즘에 걸린 다리에서 느껴지는 모진 통증

his limbs, / but he only drew his breath hard / and bent his
으로,   하지만 숨을 깊이 들이쉬고

stout neck, / and trod onward / with steady patience.
튼튼한 목을 숙인 채, 계속해서 발을 내디뎠다   한결같은 인내심으로.

unquestioning 의심하지 않는 | willow 버드 나무 | division 둑 | obliterate 지우다 | fain [고어, 시어] 기꺼이 |
lumber 우루루하며 움직이다 | a great deal 상당한 | onward 앞으로

"Rest thee at home, / Patrasche / — it is time thou didst
"집에서 쉬도록 해.   파트라슈   — 이제 정말 쉬어야 할 때가 되었어 —

rest — / and I can quite well push in the cart / by myself,"
나도 거뜬히 수레를 끌 수 있어   혼자서도,"

/ urged Nello / many a morning; / but Patrasche, / who
넬로가 설득했다   아침마다;   하지만 파트라슈는,

understood him aright, / would no more have consented /
넬로의 마음을 이해했지만,   따르려 하지 않았다

to stay at home / than a veteran soldier to shirk / when the
집에 머물라는 말을   마치 베테랑 병사가 게으름을 피우지 않듯이

charge was sounding; / and every day / he would rise / and
돌격 명령을 듣고;   그리고 매일   자리에서 일어나

place himself in his shafts, / and plod along / over the snow
수레의 손잡이 안에 서서,   터벅터벅 걸어갔다   눈 위를

/ through the fields / that his four round feet had left their
벌판을 가로질러   그의 동그란 네 발자국을 남겨왔던

print upon / so many, many years.
              수많은 세월 동안.

"One must never rest / till one dies," / thought Patrasche; /
"절대 쉬어서는 안 돼   죽을 때까지,"   파트라슈는 생각했다;

and sometimes / it seemed to him that / that time of rest for
그리고 때로는   그에게 느껴졌다   자신이 쉬게 될 그 날이

him / was not very far off. His sight was less clear / than it
그리 멀지 않았음을.   파트라슈의 시력은 희미해졌고

had been, / and it gave him pain / to rise after the night's
예전보다,   고통을 주었다   간밤의 잠자리에서 일어나는 일이,

sleep, / though he would never lie / a moment / in his straw
              비록 누워 본 적은 없었지만   잠시라도   잠자리에

/ when once the bell of the chapel tolling five / let him
      성당의 종이 다섯 번 울려   알려 주기만 하면

know / that the daybreak of labor had begun.
              하루 일과가 시작되었음을.

consent 허락하다 | shirk 게으름을 피우다, 꾀부리다 | shaft 손잡이 | toll 울리다 | stroke 손길 | withered 나이
든, 쭈글쭈글한 | crust 조각

"My poor Patrasche, / we shall soon lie quiet / together, /
"가여운 파트라슈,　　　　우리는 곧 조용히 눕게 되겠구나　　함께,

you and I," / said old Jehan Daas, / stretching out / to stroke
너와 나는,"　　예한 다스 할아버지는 말했다,　　손을 뻗어

the head of Patrasche / with the old withered hand / which
파트라슈의 머리를 쓰다듬으며,　늙고 쭈글쭈글한 손으로

had always shared with him / its one poor crust of bread;
언제나 나누어 주었던　　　변변치 못한 빵 한 조각이라도;

/ and the hearts of the old man and the old dog / ached
그리고 할아버지와 늙은 개의 마음은

together / with one thought: / When they were gone, / who
함께 아팠다　한 가지 생각으로:　그들이 세상을 떠나면,

would care for their darling?
누가 사랑스런 넬로를 돌봐줄까?

Key Expression

by oneself : 홀로, 혼자서

by oneself는 alone의 의미를 지닌 숙어입니다. 이처럼 전치사와 재귀대명
사가 결합한 다양한 숙어 표현을 알아볼까요.

▶by oneself : 홀로, 혼자서(=alone)
▶for oneself : 혼자의 힘으로(=without anyone's help)
▶of oneself : 저절로
▶beside oneself : 제정신이 아닌
▶to oneself : 혼자 차지하는, 독점하는
▶in spite of oneself : 자신도 모르게
▶in itself : 그 자체에, 본래
▶between ourselves : 우리끼리 이야기인데, 비밀 이야기인데

ex) I can quite well push in the cart by myself.
　　나 혼자서도 수레를 잘 밀 수 있어.

One afternoon, / as they came back / from Antwerp / over
어느 날 오후,　　　넬로와 파트라슈가 돌아오는 길에　안트베르펜으로부터

the snow, / which had become hard and smooth / as marble
눈 위를,　　딱딱하고 미끄럽게 펼쳐져 있었던　　　　　대리석처럼

/ over all the Flemish plains, / they found dropped in the
안트베르펜의 모든 들판 위에,　　　그들은 땅에 떨어진 것을 발견했다,

road / a pretty little puppet, / a tambourine — player, / all
예쁘고 작은 인형이었다,　　탬버린을 치는 모습의,　　전체가

scarlet and gold, / about six inches high, / and, / unlike
주홍색과 금색으로 되어 있고,　길이는 6인치 정도였으며,　그리고,

greater personages / when Fortune lets them drop, / quite
유명 인사들과는 달리　　하늘에 버림받았을 때의,

unspoiled and unhurt / by its fall. It was a pretty toy. Nello
망가지도 다치지도 않는 것이었다　떨어졌음에도,　예쁜 장난감이었다.

tried to find its owner, / and, / failing, / thought / that it was
넬로는 주인을 찾아주려 했다,　하지만,　실패하자,　생각했다　그것이 딱 좋은

just the thing / to please Alois.
물건이라고　　알루아를 기쁘게 해 주기에.

It was quite night / when he passed the mill-house: /
깊은 밤이었다   그가 방앗간을 지나칠 때에는:

he knew / the little window of her room. It could be no
그는 알았다   알루아 방의 작은 창문이 있는 것을.   나쁜 일은 없을 것이라고,

harm, / he thought, / if he gave her / his little piece of
그는 생각했다,   만약 알루아에게 준다고 해도

treasure-trove, / they had been playfellows / so long.
자신이 발견한 작은 장난감을,   그들은 소꿉친구로 지냈으니까   오랫동안.

There was a shed / with a sloping roof / beneath her
창고가 있었다   경사진 지붕이 있는   그녀의 여닫이 창 아래로:

casement: / he climbed it / and tapped softly / at the
          그는 그것을 기어올라가서 가볍게 톡톡 두들겼다   격자무늬 창문을:

lattice: / there was a little light within. The child opened
          안에는 희미한 불빛이 있었다.   소녀가 창문을 열었고

it / and looked out / half frightened. Nello put / the
밖을 바라 보았다   반쯤 놀란 표정으로.   넬로는 올려 놓았다

tambourine-player / into her hands. "Here is a doll / I
탬버린을 연주하는 인형을   그녀의 손 안에.   "여기 인형이야

found in the snow, / Alois. Take it," / he whispered / —
내가 눈길에서 발견한 거야,   알루아.   네가 가져,"   넬로가 속삭였다

"take it, / and God bless thee, / dear!"
— "네가 가져,   그리고 하나님이 널 축복하시길,   알루아!"

He slid down / from the shed-roof / before she had time
넬로는 미끄러져 내려와서 창고의 지붕에서   그녀가 고맙다는 말을 하기도 전에,

to thank him, / and ran off / through the darkness.
달아나 버렸다   어둠 속으로.

puppet 작은 인형 | personage 유명인사 | Fortune 하늘, 운명 | unspoiled 망가진 | unhurt 상처입지 않은 |
treasure-trove 발견물 | lattice 격자무늬

A. 다음 문장을 해석해 보세요.

(1) He had gone without bread / many a time / to procure even the few rude vehicles / that he had here.
→

(2) Patrasche had lain quiet / countless hours / watching its gradual creation / after the labor of each day was done.
→

(3) The drawings were to go in / on the first day of December, / and the decision be given / on the twenty-fourth, / so that he who should win / might rejoice / with all his people / at the Christmas season.
→

(4) Hard work, / especially for Patrasche, / for the passage of the years, / that were only bringing Nello a stronger youth, / were bringing him / old age,
→

B. 다음 주어진 문장이 되도록 빈칸에 써 넣으세요.

(1) 그는 <u>자신의 머리 속을 사로잡은 수없이 많은 환상 가운데 하나</u>에 형체를 부여했다.

He had given shape to ▭

▭.

(2) 그는 저녁에 여러 번 <u>나무꾼인 마이클 할아버지가 그렇게 앉아 있는 것을 본 적이 있었다.</u>

▭ at evening many a time.

(3) <u>그가 허락하고 받아들인 것은</u> 뒤에서 트럭을 밀어주는 도움을 받는 것 뿐이었다.

▭ was the help of a thrust from behind to the truck.

(4) 때로는 자신이 쉬게 될 그때가 그리 멀지 않은 것 같아 보였다.

Sometimes it seemed to him that ▭▭▭▭▭▭▭
▭▭▭▭▭▭▭▭▭▭▭▭.

C. 다음 주어진 문구가 알맞은 문장이 되도록 순서를 맞춰 보세요.

(1) 그가 자신이 본 것을 표현할 수 있는 방법은 단지 검은 색이나 흰 색 뿐이었다.
(the things / he / he / could / saw / fashion)
It was only in black or white that ▭▭▭▭▭▭▭
▭▭▭▭▭▭▭.

(2) 누구도 아무 것도 그에게 가르쳐 준 적이 없었다.
(ever / anything / had / No one / him / taught)
→

(3) 나는 혼자서도 거뜬히 수레를 끌 수 있어.
(myself / can / in the cart / quite well / I / by / push)
→

(4) 그들이 세상을 떠나면, 누가 그들의 사랑스런 아이를 돌봐줄까?
(who / were gone, / would / When / they / their darling? / care for)
→

D. 다음 단어에대한맞는 설명과 연결해 보세요.

(1) anatomy   ▶   ◀ ① bfeel great love and admiration

(2) mournful   ▶   ◀ ② the study of the structure of the bodies

(3) adore   ▶   ◀ ③ agree to do something

(4) consent   ▶   ◀ ④ very sad

6

That night / there was a fire at the mill. Outbuildings and
그날 밤   방앗간에 불이 났다.   별채들과 많은 옥수수들이

much corn were destroyed, / although the mill itself and
타 버렸다,   비록 방앗간과 주택은

the dwelling-house / were unharmed.
                     해를 입지 않았지만.

All the village was out / in terror, / and engines came
모든 마을 사람들은 밖으로 나왔고 겁에 질려,   소방차들이 신속히 달려왔다

tearing / through the snow / from Antwerp. The miller
        눈길을 뚫고   안트베르펜으로부터.   방앗간 주인은 보험에

was insured, / and would lose nothing: / nevertheless, / he
가입되어 있어서,   손해 볼 것은 전혀 없었다: 그럼에도 불구하고,

was in furious wrath, / and declared aloud / that the fire
그는 몹시 분노하며,   큰 소리로 선언했다   그 화재는

was / due to no accident, / but to some foul intent.
사고로 일어난 것이 아니라,   사악한 의도로 인한 것이라고.

Key Expression

due to : ~ 때문에, ~로 인하여

due to는 '~때문에'라는 의미로 because of와 같은 뜻의 표현입니다. 비슷한 표현으로 owing to가 있습니다. due to는 because of에 비해 문어체에서 자주 쓰입니다.

due to나 owing to가 사고나 안 좋은 일의 원인에 주로 쓰이는 표현이라면, thanks to는 좋은 일에 원인에 쓰이는 표현으로 '~덕분에'라고 해석합니다.

ex) The fire was due to no accident, but to some foul intent.
    그 화재는 사고로 인한 것이 아니라, 사악한 의도로 인한 것이었다.

oubuilding 별채 | dwelling-house 주택 | tearing 냅다, 쏜살같이 | thrust 밀다 | loiter 어슬렁거리다 | on one's soul 진심으로 | jest 농담 | openly 터놓고, 드러내 놓고 | charge 혐의 | bruit 유포하다 | grudge 원한, 유감 | intercourse 교제 | landowner 지주 | secure 얻어내다, 지키다

Nello, / awakened from his sleep, / ran to help / with the
넬로도,　잠에서 깨어나서,　도우려 달려갔다　.다른 사람들과

rest: / Baas Cogez thrust him / angrily / aside. "Thou
함께:　코제 나리는 그를 밀어붙였다　화를 내며　한쪽으로.

wert loitering here / after dark," / he said roughly. "I
"네가 이곳을 어슬렁거렸지　어두워진 후,"　그는 거칠게 말했다.

believe, / on my soul, / that thou dost know / more of the
"내 생각에는,　진심으로,　네가 알고 있을 거야　이 화재에 대해서

fire / than any one."
어느 누구보다도."

Nello heard him / in silence, / stupefied, / not supposing
넬로는 그의 말을 들었다　잠자코,　어안이 벙벙해서,　생각도 못 했으니까

/ that anyone could say such things / except in jest, / and
누군가 그런 말을 하리라고　농담이 아니고서야,

not comprehending / how anyone could pass a jest / at
그리고 이해할 수 없었으니까　어떻게 농담을 던질 수 있는지

such a time.
그런 상황에서.

Nevertheless, / the miller said / the brutal thing / openly /
그럼에도 불구하고,　방앗간 주인은 말했다　그런 잔혹한 말을　공개적으로

to many of his neighbors / in the day that followed; / and
많은 이웃들에게　바로 그 다음 날;

though no serious charge / was ever preferred / against
비록 심각한 혐의를　씌우려 한 것은 아니었지만

the lad, / it got bruited / about that Nello had been seen /
소년에게,　그 소문은 퍼져 나갔다　넬로가 목격되었다고

in the mill-yard / after dark / on some unspoken errand,
방앗간 마당에서　어두워지고 나서　은밀한 의도를 가지고,

/ and that he bore Baas Cogez a grudge / for forbidding
그리고 넬로가 코제 나리에게 원한을 품고 있다고　금지한 것에 대해서

/ his intercourse with little Alois; / and so the hamlet,
알루아와의 교제를;　그래서 그렇게 마을 사람들은,

/ which followed the sayings / of its richest landowner
말을 따랐다　가장 부자인 지주의

/ servilely, / and whose families / all hoped to secure /
굽실거리며,　또한 마을의 가족들은　모두 차지하겠다는 희망을 갖고 있는

the riches of Alois / in some future time / for their sons,
알루아의 재물을　　　　미래에　　　　　아들들을 위해서,

/ took the hint / to give grave looks / and cold words / to
눈치를 채고　　　매몰찬 표정을 지으며　　쌀쌀맞게 대했다

old Jehan Daas's grandson. No one said anything to him
예한 다스 할아버지의 손자에게.　　아무도 넬로에게 아무 말도 하지 않았지만

/ openly, / but all the village agreed together / to humor
대놓고,　　하지만 모든 주민들은 일제히 동의했다　　　비위를 맞추는데

/ the miller's prejudice, / and at the cottages and farms
방앗간 주인의 억지 주장에,　　그리고 농가와 농장들에서는

/ where Nello and Patrasche called / every morning /
넬로와 파트라슈가 불려 다녔던　　　매일 아침

for the milk / for Antwerp, / downcast glances and brief
우유를 모으기 위해　안트베르펜으로 싣고 가는,　업신여기는 시선과 짧은 말을

phrases / replaced to them / the broad smiles and cheerful
　　　그들에게 대신 전했다　　환한 미소와 유쾌한 환영 인사가 아니라

greetings / to which they had been always used. No one
　　　그들이 항상 사용했었던.　　　　아무도 정말로

really credited / the miller's absurd suspicion, / nor the
믿지는 않았다　　　방앗간 주인의 터무니없는 의심이나,

outrageous accusations / born of them, / but the people
말도 안 되는 트집을　　　그들에 대해 만들어진,　다만 사람들은

were / all very poor / and very ignorant, / and the one rich
모두 너무 가난했고　매우 무지했으며,　　　동네의 유일한 부자가

man of the place / had pronounced / against him.
　　　말했기 때문이었다　넬로에 반대하는 말을.

Nello, / in his innocence and his friendlessness, / had no
넬로는,　　순진했고 자기 편도 없었기에,

strength to stem / the popular tide.
저지할 힘도 없었다　　대다수 사람들의 태도를.

humor 비위를 맞추다 | prejudice 편견 | downcast 눈을 내리뜬 | absurd 터무니 없는 | suspicion 혐의 |
outrageous 아주 별난, 터무니 없는 | accusation 고발, 혐의 | ignorant 무지한 | pronounce 공표하다 | stem
저지하다

90　A Dog of Flanders

"Thou art very cruel / to the lad," / the miller's wife dared
"당신은 너무 잔혹해요   그 소년에게," 방앗간 주인의 부인이 용기 내어 말했다.

to say, / weeping, / to her lord. "Sure / he is an innocent
울면서,   남편에게.   "분명, 그 애는 순진하고

lad / and a faithful, / and would never dream of / any such
믿을 만한 아이라서,   꿈도 꾸지 못할 거예요

wickedness, / however sore / his heart might be."
그런 사악한 행동은,   아무리 아프더라도   그의 마음이."

But Baas Cogez being an obstinate man, / having once said
하지만 코제 나리는 고집 센 사람이어서,   한 번 뱉은 말에 대해서

a thing / held to it doggedly, / though in his innermost soul
끈덕지게 집착했다,   비록 마음속 깊은 곳에서는

/ he knew well / the injustice / that he was committing.
그도 잘 알고 있었지만   옳지 못한 일을   저지르고 있다는 것을.

Meanwhile, / Nello endured the injury / done against him /
그러는 동안,   넬로는 상처를 견뎌 냈다   자신이 당한

with a certain proud patience / that disdained to complain:
자존심 강한 인내심으로   불평하기를 거부하며:

/ he only gave way a little / when he was quite alone / with
그는 조금 드러냈을 뿐이다   조용히 혼자 있었을 때에만

old Patrasche. Besides, / he thought, / "If it should win!
늙은 파트라슈와 함께.   또한,   그는 생각했다,   "내 그림이 상을 받는다면!

They will be sorry / then, / perhaps."
모두 미안해 할 거야   그때가 되면, 아마도."

Still, / to a boy not quite sixteen, / and who had dwelt / in
그럼에도, 열 여섯 살도 안 된 소년에게는,   살아온

one little world / all his short life, / and in his childhood
작은 세계에서   짧은 세월 동안,   그리고 어린 시절에

/ had been caressed and applauded / on all sides, / it was
사랑 받고 칭찬 받았던   모든 면에서,   그것은 힘든

a hard trial / to have the whole of / that little world turn
시련이었다   전부를 감당하는 것은   그 작은 세상이 자신을 등졌다는 사실을

against him / for naught. Especially hard / in that bleak,
부당하게.   특별히 힘들었다   눈보라가 휘몰아치는 시기에,

snow-bound, / famine-stricken winter-time, / when /
배고픔으로 허덕이는 겨울철,   그때에는

the only light and warmth there / could be found / abode
빛과 온기는 오직 그곳에서만   찾을 수 있었으니까

beside the village hearths / and in the kindly greetings / of
마을 사람들의 온정과   친절한 인사말 속에서만

neighbors. In the winter-time / all drew nearer to each other,
이웃들의.   겨울철이 되자   모두가 가깝게 지냈다.

/ all to all, / except to Nello and Patrasche, / with whom
다들 서로서로,   넬로와 파트라슈를 제외하고,   이제는 아무도

none now / would have anything to do, / and who were left
무슨 일이든 하려 하지 않았다,   그래서 넬로와 파트라슈는 남겨졌다

to / fare as they might / with the old paralyzed, / bedridden
살아가도록   늙고 병들어,   누워 있는 노인과

man / in the little cabin, / whose fire was often low, / and
작은 오두막집에,   그리고 오두막의 불꽃은 자주 사그러들었고,

whose board was often without bread, / for there was a
찬장에는 빵이 없는 날이 많았다,   왜냐하면 안트베르펜에서

buyer from Antwerp / who had taken to drive his mule in
온 수집상이 있어서   노새를 몰고 와서

/ of a day / for the milk of the various dairies, / and there
어느 날   우유와 유제품들을 거두어 갔고,

were only three or four of the people / who had refused
겨우 서너 사람만이   그의 거래 조건을 거절하고

his terms of purchase / and remained faithful / to the little
신의를 지켰기 때문에   작은 녹색 수레에.

green cart. So that / the burden which Patrasche drew /
그렇게 해서   파트라슈가 감당해야 하는 부담은

had become very light, / and the centime-pieces in Nello's
매우 가벼워졌지만,   넬로의 호주머니에 들어가는 동전들도

pouch / had become, / alas! / Very small / likewise.
변했다,   아아!   매우 줄어든 것이다   마찬가지로.

---

obstinate 고집이 센 | doggedly 끈덕지게 | innermost 가장 안쪽의, 내밀한 | injustice 부당함 | commit
저지르다 | disdain 거부하다, 무시하다 | applaud 박수를 치다, 갈채를 보내다 | turn against ~에게 등을 돌리다
| naught 0, 무가치, 사악한 | snow-bound 눈에 갇힌 | famine 기근 | fare (고어) 살아가다, 지내다 | bedridden
아파서 누워 있는 | mule 노새 | dairy 유제품 | centime 상팀, 프랑스의 화폐 단위, 1/100 프랑

93

The dog would stop, / as usual, / at all the familiar gates, /
파트라슈는 멈춰 서서, 평소처럼, 낯익은 대문들마다,

which were now closed to him, / and look up at them / with
이제 굳게 닫혀 버린, 문들을 쳐다보았다 애석한

wistful, / mute appeal; / and it cost the neighbors a pang /
표정으로, 말없이 호소하며; 그리고 이웃들에게도 고통스러운 일이었다

to shut their doors and their hearts, / and let Patrasche draw
자신들의 문과 마음을 걸어 잠궈 버려서, 파트라슈가 끌고 가게 하는 것이

/ his cart on again, / empty. Nevertheless, / they did it, / for
수레를 다시, 비어 있는 채로. 그럼에도 불구하고, 그들은 계속했다,

they desired to please Baas Cogez.
코제 나리를 기쁘게 하고 싶었기에.

Noël was close at hand.
크리스마스가 코 앞으로 다가왔다.

The weather was very wild and cold. The snow was six feet
날씨는 몹시 혹독하고 추웠다. 눈은 6피트까지 쌓였고,

deep, / and the ice was firm / enough to bear oxen and men
얼음이 꽁꽁 얼어서 황소나 사람이 밟고 다녀도 될 정도였다

upon it / everywhere. At this season / the little village was
어디든지. 이런 계절이면 이 작은 마을은

/ always gay and cheerful. At the poorest dwelling / there
항상 즐겁고 활기가 넘쳤다. 가장 가난한 집이라도

were *possets and cakes, / joking and dancing, / sugared
파시트와 케이크가 있었고, 농담을 주고 받으며 춤을 췄고, 설탕을 뿌린 성자

saints and gilded Jésus. The merry Flemish bells / jingled
상과 금박을 입힌 예수님상도 있었다. 경쾌한 플란다스의 종소리가 곳곳에서

everywhere / on the horses; / everywhere within doors
딸랑딸랑 울렸다 말의 목에 달린; 어느 집이든 그 안에는

/ some well-filled soup-pot / sang and smoked / over the
수프가 가득 찬 솥단지들이 보글보글 노래하며 김을 뿜어냈다

stove; / and everywhere over the snow / without laughing
화덕 위에서; 그리고 어느 곳이나 눈길 위에서는 웃음 소리가 없는

/ maidens pattered / in bright kerchiefs and stout kirtles, /
소녀들이 종종걸음으로 걸어갔다 밝은 색의 스카프와 튼튼한 가운을 두르고,

* 뜨거운 우유에 술과 설탕을 넣은 음료

going to and from the mass. Only in the little hut / it was
미사를 보러 갔다.   오직 그 작은 오두막만이

very dark and very cold.
매우 어둡고 추웠다.

apeal 호소하다 | maiden 소녀 | kerchief 스카프 | kirtle 가운

Nello and Patrasche were left / utterly alone, / for one night
넬로와 파트라슈는 남겨졌다   완전히 홀로,   왜냐하면 어느 날 밤

/ in the week before the Christmas Day, / Death entered
크리스마스를 일 주일 앞둔,   죽음이 찾아와서,

there, / and took away from life forever old Jehan Daas,
예한 다스 할아버지의 생명을 영원히 앗아갔기 때문이었다.

/ who had never known life / aught save its poverty and
할아버지는 모르고 살았다   가난과 고통 밖에는.

its pains. He had long been half dead, / incapable of any
그는 오랜 세월동안 반쯤 죽은 상태였다,   움직이지도 못하고

movement / except a feeble gesture, / and powerless for
아주 연약한 몸짓 말고는,   기력도 없는 채로

anything / beyond a gentle word; / and yet / his loss fell
다정한 말을 건네는 것 밖에는: 그렇지만   그의 죽음은 둘 모두를

on them both / with a great horror in it: / they mourned
빠뜨렸다   엄청난 공포에: 그들은 정성을 다해

him passionately. He had passed away from them / in
할아버지를 애도했다.   할아버지는 그들 곁을 떠났고

his sleep, / and when in the gray dawn / they learned /
잠든 사이에,   그래서 새벽이 밝아올 때쯤   알게 되자

their bereavement, / unutterable solitude and desolation /
가족을 잃었다는 사실을,   말로 표현할 수 없는 고독과 적막함이

seemed to close around them. He had long been / only a
그들 주위로 몰려드는 것 같았다.   할아버지는 오랫동안

poor, feeble, paralyzed old man, / who could not raise a
가난하고, 연약하고, 불구인 노인일 뿐이어서,   손을 들어 줄 수도 없었지만

hand / in their defence, / but he had loved them well: / his
그들을 지켜주기 위해,   그들을 매우 사랑했다:

smile had always welcomed / their return.
항상 미소로 맞이했다   그들이 돌아올 때면.

---

utterly 완전히 | aught 어떤 것(=anything) | incapable 무능한, 하지 못하는 | powerless 힘없는, 무력한 | mourn
애도하다, 슬퍼하다 | pass away 죽다 | bereavement 사별, (가족의) 사망 | unutterable 말로 표현할 수 없는
| solitude 고독 | desolation 적막함 | deal 널판 | nameless 이름 없는 | relent 수그러들다 | immortelles
건조화, 마른 꽃(국화 등) | mound: 흙무더기, 무덤 | displace 옮겨 놓다, 대신 들어서다

They mourned for him / unceasingly, / refusing to be
그들은 할아버지를 위해 흐느꼈다   끊임없이,   위로 받기를 거부하고,

comforted, / as in the white winter day / they followed
흰 눈이 내린 겨울 날   할아버지의 관을 따라

the deal shell / that held his body / to the nameless grave /
할아버지의 육신이 들어 있는   이름 없는 무덤까지 가면서

by the little gray church. They were his only mourners, /
작은 회색 성당 옆에 있는.   그들이 유일한 장례 행렬이었다,

these two / whom he had left friendless / upon earth / —
그 둘이   외톨이로 남겨진   이 세상에

the young boy and the old dog.
— 어린 소년과 늙은 개가 전부였다.

"Surely, / he will relent now / and let the poor lad come
"분명히,   남편도 이제 마음이 누그러져서   그 불쌍한 소년을 오게 하겠지

/ hither?" / thought the miller's wife, / glancing at her
이곳으로?"   방앗간 주인의 부인은 생각하며,   남편을 힐끗 보았다

husband / smoking by the hearth.
난로가에서 담배를 피우고 있던.

Baas Cogez knew her thought, / but he hardened his heart,
코제 나리는 아내의 생각을 알고 있었지만,   마음을 다잡아 먹고,

/ and would not unbar his door / as the little, humble
문의 빗장을 풀지 않았다   작고, 초라한 장례 행렬이 지나가는 동안.

funeral went by. "The boy is a beggar," / he said to
"저 녀석은 거지야."   그는 스스로에게 말했다:

himself: / "he shall not be about Alois."
"알루아 곁에는 얼씬도 해서는 안 돼."

The woman dared not say anything / aloud, / but when the
부인은 감히 아무 말도 할 수 없었지만   큰 소리를 내어,

grave was closed / and the mourners had gone, / she put a
무덤이 흙으로 덮이고   장례 행렬이 떠나자,

wreath of immortelles / into Alois's hands / and bade her
마른 국화 꽃으로 만든 화환을 주며   알루아의 손에   그녀에게 시켰다

/ go and lay it reverently / on the dark, unmarked mound /
가서 그 꽃을 소중하게 놓고 오라고   어둡고, 묘비도 없는 흙무더기에

where the snow was displaced.
눈에 덮여 가려진.

 mini test 6

A. 다음 문장을 해석해 보세요.

(1) He was in furious wrath, / and declared aloud / that the fire
was / due to no accident, / but to some foul intent.
→

(2) I believe, / on my soul, / that thou dost know / more of the fire
/ than any one.

→

(3) No one said anything to him / openly, / but all the village
agreed together / to humor / the miller's prejudice.
→

(4) He is an innocent lad / and a faithful, / and would never dream
of / any such wickedness, / however sore / his heart might be.
→

B. 다음 주어진 문구가 알맞은 문장이 되도록 순서를 맞춰보세요.

(1) 그 일은 이웃들에게 아픔을 안겨 줬다.
(a / cost / the neighbors / pang / It)
→

(2) 크리스마스가 코 앞으로 다가왔다.
(was / Noel / at / hand / close)
→

(3) 그는 <u>아주 연약한 몸짓 외에는 움직이지도 못한 채</u> 오랜 세월 동안 반쯤 죽은 상
태였다
(any / feeble / incapable / except / a / gesture / movement / of)
He had long been half dead,

.

 Answer

A. (1) 그는 몹시 분노하며 그 화재는 사고로 일어난 것이 아니라 사악한 의도에 의한 것이라고 큰 소리로
선언했다. (2) 나는 진심으로 네가 이 화재에 대해서 어느 누구보다도 잘 알고 있을 거라고 생각해. (3) 아무
도 넬로에게 대놓고 무슨 말을 한 건 아니었지만 모든 마을 사람들은 방앗간 주인의 억지 주장에 비위를

A Dog of Flanders

(4) 그는 잠든 상태로 그들 곁을 떠났다.
(away / sleep / He / passed / had / from / in / his / them)
→

C. 다음 주어진 문장이 본문의 내용과 맞으면 T, 틀리면 F에 동그라미 하세요.

(1) Nello was suspected of setting fire.
(T / F)

(2) After the fire, the milk cart of Patrasche became lighter.
(T / F)

(3) There were so many people at the funeral.
(T / F)

(4) Alois' mother let her put a wreath of immortelles on the grave.
(T / F)

D. 의미가 서로 비슷한 것끼리 연결해 보세요.

(1) declare   ▶   ◀ ① bias
(2) prejudice   ▶   ◀ ② desolation
(3) obstinate   ▶   ◀ ③ pronounce
(4) solitude   ▶   ◀ ④ stubborn

 7

Nello and Patrasche went home / with broken hearts. But
넬로와 파트라슈는 집으로 돌아왔다   마음에 깊은 상처를 안고.

even of that poor, melancholy, cheerless home / they were
하지만 그 가난하고, 슬픈, 썰렁한 집에서조차

denied the consolation. There was a month's rent over-due
위안을 얻을 수 없었다.   한 달치 집세가 밀려 있었고

/ for their little home, / and when Nello had paid / the last
그 작은 집에 대해.   넬로가 지불하자   마지막

sad service to the dead / he had not a coin left. He went
고인을 위한 장례 비용으로   그에게는 동전 한 푼도 남지 않았다.   넬로는 찾아가서

and begged / grace of the owner of the hut, / a cobbler /
간청했다   오두막의 집 주인에게 은혜를 베풀어 달라고,   구두 수선공인

who went every Sunday night / to drink his *pint of wine
매주 일요일 밤마다 가던   포도주를 마시고 담배를 피우러

and smoke / with Baas Cogez. The cobbler would grant no
피우러   코제 나리와.   구두 수선공은 자비를 베풀려 하지 않았다.

mercy. He was a harsh, miserly man, / and loved money.
                    그는 냉혹하고, 인색한 사람이었고,   돈을 사랑했다.

He claimed / in default of his rent / every stick and stone,
그는 요구했다   집세의 대가로   모든 나무토막과 돌멩이 하나까지,

/ every pot and pan, / in the hut, / and bade Nello and
또한 모든 솥과 냄비를,   오두막에 있는,   그리고 넬로와 파트라슈에게 명령했다

Patrasche / be out of it / on the morrow.
집에서 나가라고   그 다음 날 당장.

Now, / the cabin was lowly enough, / and in some sense /
이제,   그 오두막은 충분히 초라했고,   어떤 면에서는

miserable enough, / and yet their hearts clove to it / with
처참하기까지 했다.   그렇지만 그들은 그 집에 애착을 가지고 있었다

a great affection. They had been so happy there, / and in
매우 큰 애정으로.   그들은 그곳에서 매우 행복했었다.

the summer, / with its clambering vine / and its flowering
여름이면,   포도 넝쿨이 벽을 타고 오르며   꽃 핀 강낭콩이 넝쿨과 어우러져,

beans, / it was so pretty and bright / in the midst of the
                그 광경은 매우 아름답고 눈부셨다   햇살 가득한 들판 가운데 있는!

sunlighted fields!

There life in it / had been full of labor and privation, /
그곳에서의 삶은   고된 일과 가난으로 가득했지만,

and yet / they had been so well content, / so gay of heart,
그래도   그들은 아주 만족했고,   진심으로 즐거웠다.

/ running together to meet / the old man's never-failing
함께 만나러 달려가면서   항상 미소로 반겨주는 할아버지를!

smile of welcome!

All night long / the boy and the dog / sat by the fireless
밤새도록   소년과 개는   불기 없는 난로 부근에 앉아서

hearth / in the darkness, / drawn close together / for
어둠 속에서,   서로를 꼭 껴안고

warmth and sorrow. Their bodies were insensible to the
온기와 슬픔을 나누었다.   그들의 몸은 추위로 감각을 잃었지만,

cold, / but their hearts seemed frozen / in them.
심장은 꽁꽁 얼어버린 듯 했다   그들의 몸 안에서.

When the morning broke / over the white, chill earth / it
날이 밝았을 때는   하얗고 쌀쌀한 대지 위로

was the morning of Christmas Eve. With a shudder, / Nello
크리스마스 이브의 아침이었다.   덜덜 떨면서,

clasped close to him / his only friend, / while his tears
넬로는 그를 꼭 껴안았다   하나뿐인 친구를,   뜨거운 눈물을 뚝뚝 흘리면서

fell hot and fast / on the dog's frank forehead. "Let us go,
개의 숨김 없는 이마 위로.   "파트라슈, 가자

Patrasche / — dear, dear Patrasche," / he murmured. "We
— 사랑하는, 내 사랑하는 파트라슈,"   넬로는 작은 소리로 말했다.

will not wait / to be kicked out: / let us go."
"기다리지 말자   쫓겨날 때까지: 가자."

---

* 파인트, 영국에서는 0.568 리터, 다른 국가와 미국에서는 0.473리터

over-due 기한이 지난 | cobbler 구두 수선공 | lowly 낮은, 하찮은 | cleave 집착하다 | privation 궁핍 |
never-failing 변하지 않는 | chill 한기 | shudder 몸을 떨다 | clasp 꼭 껴안다, 움켜쥐다 | frank 솔직한 | kick
out 쫓아내다

Patrasche had no will / but his, / and they went sadly, / side
파트라슈는 자신의 의지가 아닌   넬로의 의지를 따랐고, 둘은 슬프게 떠나,

by side, / out from the little place / which was so dear to
나란히,   작은 오두막을 나왔다   그 둘에게는 매우 소중한,

them both, / and in which every humble, homely thing was
그곳에 있는 모든 초라하고, 소박한 것은

/ to them precious and beloved. Patrasche drooped his head
그들에게는 소중하고 사랑스러운 것이었다.   파트라슈는 힘없이 고개를 떨구었다

wearily / as he passed by / his own green cart: / it was no
지나갈 때   자신의 녹색 수레를: 이제 그것은 더 이상

longer his / — it had to go with the rest / to pay the rent, /
그의 것이 아니었다 — 그것 역시 나머지와 같이 보내야 했다   집세를 갚기 위해서,

and his brass harness / lay idle and glittering / on the snow.
그리고 그의 놋쇠로 만든 마구도   반짝거리며 뒹굴고 있었다   흰 눈 위에서.

The dog could have / lain down beside it and died / for very
파트라슈는 할 수 있다면   그 곁에 드러누워 죽고 싶었지만

heart-sickness / as he went, / but whilst the lad lived / and
비통한 마음에   떠나갈 때,   소년이 살아 있는 동안   그리고 자신

needed him / Patrasche would not yield and give way.
을 필요로 하는 한   파트라슈는 굴복하거나 무너지지 않으려 했다.

They took the old accustomed road / into Antwerp. The
그들은 오래된 익숙한 길을 걸어갔다   안트베르펜으로 이어진.

day had yet scarce more than dawned, / most of the shutters
아직 동이 트기 전 이른 새벽이라,   대부분의 덧문들은

/ were still closed, / but some of the villagers were about.
아직 닫혀 있었지만,   몇몇 주민들은 막 깨어난 참이었다.

They took no notice / whilst the dog and the boy passed
그들은 알아채지 못했다   소년과 개가 그들을 지나갈 때에도.

by them. At one door / Nello paused / and looked wistfully
한 문 앞에서   넬로는 멈춰 서서   안타까운 눈빛으로 안을 들여다

within: / his grandfather had done / many a kindly turn / in
보았다: 그의 할아버지가 베풀었던   많은 친절을

neighbor's service / to the people who dwelt there.
이웃에 대한 봉사로   그 집에 사는 사람들에게.

"Would you give Patrasche a crust?" / he said, timidly.
"파트라슈에게 빵 조각이라도 주시겠어요?" 넬로가 소심하게 말했다.

"He is old, / and he has had nothing / since last forenoon."
"나이가 많은데, 아무것도 먹지를 못했어요. 어제 아침부터 쭉."

The woman shut the door hastily, / murmuring some
그 집 여자는 문을 서둘러 닫았다. 애매모호하게 중얼거리며

vague saying / about wheat and rye being very dear / that
  밀과 호밀이 아주 귀하다고 이번

season. The boy and the dog / went on again wearily: /
겨울에는. 소년과 개는 맥없이 다시 길을 떠났다:

they asked no more.
그리고는 더 이상 부탁하지 않았다.

By slow and painful ways / they reached Antwerp / as the
느리고 힘겹게 그들은 안트베르펜에 도착했다

chimes tolled ten.
종소리가 10시를 알릴 무렵.

Key Expression 🍋

no more와 no longer

no more는 '그 이상 ~하지 않다', no longer는 '더 이상 ~아닌/~하지 않는'
의 의미를 가진 말로, 각각 not ~ any more, not ~ any longer로 바꾸어
쓸 수 있습니다.
이 두 개의 숙어는 비슷한 의미를 가지고 있으나 어감의 차이가 있습니다. no
more는 더 이상의 양을 이야기할 때, 혹은 동작을 다시 재개할 것인지의 여부
에 초점을 맞추고 있습니다. 반면 no longer의 경우에는 상태를 지속할 것인가
의 여부가 초점이 됩니다.

ex) It was no longer his — it had to go with the rest to pay the rent. (상태)
   그것은 더 이상 그의 것이 아니었다 — 그것은 집세를 갚기 위해 남은 것과 함께
   보내야만 했다.
   They asked no more. (동작)
   그들은 더 이상 부탁하지 않았다.

precious 귀중한, 소중한 | beloved 사랑하는 | droop 아래로 처지다 | glitter 반짝반짝 빛나다 | heart-sickness
비통함 | yield 굴복하다 | give way 무너지다 | vague 희미한, 모호한

"If I had anything about me / I could sell / to get him
"내게 뭐라도 있었으면   그것을 팔아서   파트라슈에게 빵을 사 줄

bread!" / thought Nello, / but he had nothing / except the
텐데!"   넬로는 생각했다.   하지만 그에게는 아무것도 없었다

wisp of linen and serge / that covered him, / and his pair
옷 조각과 외투 외에는   그가 입고 있는,

of wooden shoes. Patrasche understood, / and nestled his
그리고 나막신밖에.   파트라슈는 이해하며,   그의 코를 얹었다

nose / into the lad's hand, / as though to pray him / not to
소년의 손 안에.   마치 기도하는 듯이

be disquieted / for any woe or want of his.
불안해 하지 말라고   자신의 고통이나 필요한 것 때문에.

The winner of the drawing-prize / was to be proclaimed
미술 대회의 입상자는   정오에 발표될 예정이었다,

at noon, / and to the public building / where he had left
그렇기에 공회당으로   자신의 보물을 두고 온

his treasure / Nello made his way. On the steps / and in
넬로는 발길을 재촉했다.   계단마다

the entrance-hall / there was a crowd of youths / — some
그리고 입구의 홀에는   어린이들이 모여 있었다   — 몇몇은 자

of his age, some older, / all with parents or relatives or
신과 나이가 같거나 조금 많아 보였고,   모두가 부모나 친척, 또는 친구들과 함께였다.

friends. His heart was sick / with fear / as he went among
그는 마음이 아파서   두려움으로   그들 사이로 걸어 가는 동안,

them, / holding Patrasche close to him. The great bells
파트라슈를 꼭 붙들었다.   도시의 큰 종들이

of the city / clashed out the hour of noon / with brazen
정오를 가리키며 울렸다   큰 쇳소리를 내며.

clamor.

The doors of the inner hall were opened; / the eager,
안쪽의 회관의 문이 열렸고;   간절하게, 두근거리는

panting throng rushed in: / it was known that / the
인파가 안으로 몰려 들어갔다: 알려져 있었다

---

wisp 조각 | disquiet 불안, 동요 | woe 고민 | proclaim 선언하다, 선포하다 | clash 쨍 하는 소리를 내다,
충돌하다 | clamor 큰 소음 | panting 두근거리는 | throng 인파

selected picture / would be raised above the rest / upon a
입상한 그림은   나머지 것들 위에 높이 걸려 있다는 것을

wooden dais.
나무로 만든 단상 위에.

A mist obscured Nello's sight, / his head swam, / his limbs
두 눈에 이슬이 맺혀 넬로의 시야를 흐리게 했고,   머리 속은 빙빙 돌았으며,

almost failed him. When his vision cleared / he saw the
팔다리의 힘도 다 빠져 버렸다. 시야가 다시 맑아졌을 때

drawing raised on high: / it was not his own! A slow,
그는 높이 걸린 그림을 바라보았다: 하지만 넬로의 것이 아니었다!

sonorous voice / was proclaiming aloud / that victory had
느릿하고 낭랑한 목소리가   큰 소리로 선포했다

been adjudged / to Stephen Kiesslinger, / born in the burgh
우승은 결정됐다고   스테판 키슬링어로,   안트베르펜에서 태어난,

of Antwerp, / son of a wharfinger in that town.
그 도시의 선창 관리인의 아들인.

When Nello recovered his consciousness / he was lying /
넬로가 다시 의식을 차렸을 때   그는 누워 있었고

on the stones without, / and Patrasche was trying / with
아무것도 없는 돌바닥에,   파트라슈는 애쓰고 있었다   알고 있는

every art he knew / to call him back to life.
모든 방법을 동원하여   그를 정신 차리게 하려고.

In the distance / a throng of the youths of Antwerp / were
멀리서   안트베르펜의 소년 무리가   함성을

shouting / around their successful comrade, / and escorting
지르고 있었다   성공한 동료를 둘러싸고,   그를 호위하며

him / with acclamations / to his home upon the quay.
갈채와 함께   부두가에 있는 그의 집으로 향했다.

The boy staggered to his feet / and drew the dog / into his
넬로는 비틀거리며 일어서서   개를 끌어 안았다

embrace. "It is all over, / dear Patrasche," / he murmured
그의 품 안에.   "이제 다 끝났어,   사랑하는 파트라슈,"   그는 중얼거렸다

/ — "all over!"
— "다 끝났어!"

He rallied himself / as best he could, / for he was weak
넬로는 기운을 차렸다   있는 힘을 다해,   굶주림으로 몸이 허약해졌기 때문에,

from fasting, / and retraced his steps / to the village.
그리고 발걸음을 돌렸다   마을로.

obscure 희미한 | sonorous 낭랑한 | wharfinger 선창 주인, 관리인 | consciousness 의식 | comrade 동료
acclamation 환호, 갈채 | rally 회복하다 | fast 금식 | retrace 되짚어 가다

Patrasche paced by his side / with his head drooping / and
파트라슈는 그의 곁을 따라 걸어갔다   고개를 떨군 채   그의

his old limbs feeble / from hunger and sorrow.
늙은 다리는 허약해져 있었다   배고픔과 슬픔 때문에.

The snow was falling fast: / a keen hurricane blew / from
눈이 펑펑 내리고 있었고: 날카로운 허리케인이 불어 와서

the north: / it was bitter / as death on the plains. It took
북쪽으로부터: 더욱 끔찍했다   들판에서의 죽는 것만큼이나.

them long / to traverse the familiar path, / and the bells
오랜 시간이 걸려서   낯익은 길을 횡단했고,

were sounding four of the clock / as they approached the
종소리는 4시를 알리고 있었다   마을에 도착하자.

hamlet. Suddenly / Patrasche paused, / arrested by a scent
갑자기   파트라슈가 멈춰 서더니,   눈 속에서 나는 어떤 냄새에

in the snow, / scratched, whined, / and drew out with his
붙잡힌 듯,   땅을 긁으면서, 낑낑거리다가,   이빨로 끄집어냈다

teeth / a small case of brown leather. He held it up to Nello
갈색의 작은 가죽의 지갑을 .   그는 그것을 넬로에게 들어 보였다

/ in the darkness. Where they were / there stood a little
어둠 속에서.   그들이 있는 곳에는   작은 갈보리의 십자가가 있었고,

*Calvary, / and a lamp burned dully / under the cross: / the
등불 하나가 희미하게 타고 있었다   십자가 아래서:

boy mechanically / turned the case to the light: / on it / was
넬로는 기계적으로   그 지갑을 불빛에 비춰 보았다: 그 위에는

the name of Baas Cogez, / and within it / were notes for
코제 나리의 이름이 적혀 있었고,   그 안에는

two thousand francs.
2,000프랑의 지폐가 들어 있었다.

The sight roused the lad / a little from his stupor. He thrust
그것을 보자 넬로는   충격으로 정신이 혼미해졌다.   그는 그것을 셔츠

it in his shirt, / and stroked Patrasche / and drew him
의 주머니에 넣고,   파트라슈를 쓰다듬어 준 뒤   길을 재촉했다.

onward. The dog looked up wistfully / in his face.
파트라슈는 안타까운 표정으로 바라보았다   넬로의 얼굴을.

* 갈보리, 그리스도가 십자가에 못 박힌 곳

traverse 횡단하다, 가로지르다 | arrest by 붙잡히다 | scratch 긁다 | whine 낑낑대다 | stupor 무감각한

Nello made straight for the mill-house, / and went to the
넬로는 곧장 방앗간 집으로 향했고,   문 앞에 도착해

house-door / and struck on its panels. The miller's wife
나무 문을 두드렸다.   안주인이 문을 열었고

opened it / weeping, / with little Alois / clinging close to
눈물을 흘리면서, 어린 알루아는   어머니의 치맛자락을 꼭 붙들고

her skirts. "Is it thee, thou poor lad?" / she said kindly /
서 있었다.   "가여운 녀석, 너로구나?"   안주인이 다정하게 이야기 했다

through her tears. "Get thee gone / ere the Baas see thee.
눈물을 흘리면서.   "어서 가렴   코제 씨가 널 보기 전에.

We are in sore trouble to-night. He is out seeking / for a
오늘 저녁에 우리 집에 안 좋은 일이 생겼단다.   찾으러 나가셨어

power of money / that he has let fall / riding homeward, /
거액의 돈을   떨어뜨린   말을 타고 집에 오는 길에,

and in this snow / he never will find it; / and God knows /
하지만 이런 눈 속에서   아마도 절대 못 찾겠지;   하나님도 알다시피

it will go nigh to ruin us. It is Heaven's own judgment / for
우린 거의 파산하고 말 거야.   천벌을 받은 거야

the things / we have done to thee."
그 일 때문에   우리가 네게 저지른."

Nello put the note-case / in her hand / and called Patrasche
넬로가 지갑을 올려 놓고   안주인의 손에   파트라슈를 불러들였다

/ within the house.
집 안으로.

"Patrasche found the money / to-night," / he said quickly.
"파트라슈가 그 돈을 찾았어요   오늘 저녁에,"   넬로가 빠르게 말했다.

"Tell Baas Cogez so: / I think / he will not deny / the dog
"코제 나리께 그렇게 전해 주세요: 제 생각에는   그분도 거절하지 않으시겠죠

shelter and food / in his old age. Keep him from pursuing
먹이와 잠자리를 주는 것을   이 늙은 개에게.   이 개가 저를 따라 오지 못하게 막아 주세요,

me, / and I pray of you to be good to him."
그리고 부디 이 개에게 잘 대해 주세요."

Ere either woman or dog knew / what he meant / he had
안주인이나 개가 알아차리기도 전에   넬로가 무슨 말을 하는지

stooped and kissed Patrasche: / then closed the door
그는 몸을 구부려 파트라슈에게 입맞췄다: 그리곤 문을 서둘러 닫고,

hurriedly, / and disappeared / in the gloom of the fast —
사라졌다   빠르게 어두워지는 밤 속으로.

falling night.

The woman and the child stood speechless / with joy and
안주인과 소녀는 아무 말도 못하고 서 있었다   기쁨과 두려움에:

fear: / Patrasche vainly spent the fury of his anguish /
파트라슈는 헛되게 분노를 표출했다

against the iron-bound oak / of the barred house-door. They
쇠 장식을 단 참나무에 대고   빗장 걸린 문에.   그들은

did not dare / unbar the door / and let him forth: / they tried
감히 엄두도 내지 못했다 빗장을 풀고   파트라슈를 내보낼:

all they could / to solace him. They brought him / sweet
그들은 최대한 애썼다   파트라슈를 달래 보려고. 파트라슈에게 갖다 주었고

cakes and juicy meats; / they tempted him / with the best
달콤한 케이크와 싱싱한 고기를;   그를 설득했다   그들이 가진 가장 좋은

they had; / they tried to lure him / to abide by the warmth of
것으로;   그를 달래려고도 해 봤다   따뜻한 난로 주위에 머물도록;

the hearth; / but it was of no avail. Patrasche refused / to be
하지만 아무 소용이 없었다.   파트라슈는 거부했고

comforted / or to stir from / the barred portal.
편안하게 있기를   서성였다   빗장 걸린 문 앞에서.

---

panel 나무 판 | ere ~ 의 전에(=before,near) | nigh 거의 | ruin 망치다 | pursue 뒤쫓다 | fury 격분 | anguish
괴로움 | solace 위로 | tempt 유혹하다 | lure 유혹하다 | stir 움직이다

It was six o'clock / when from an opposite entrance / the
6시가 되자   반대편 입구로부터

miller at last came, / jaded and broken, / into his wife's
드디어 방앗간 주인이 돌아왔다,   맥이 풀리고 낙담한 채,   부인이 있는 곳으로.

presence. "It is lost forever," / he said, / with an ashen
"영원히 잃어버린 거야,"   그가 말했다,   얼굴이 잿빛으로 변한 채

cheek / and a quiver in his stern voice. "We have looked
그의 괴로움에 찬 목소리를 떨면서.   "등불을 들고 다 찾아 보았어

with lanterns / everywhere: / it is gone / — the little
모든 곳을: 하지만 사라져 버렸어

maiden's portion and all!"
— 알루아의 몫까지 모두!"

His wife put the money / into his hand, / and told him /
안주인이 그 돈을 올려 놓고   코제 씨의 손에,   그에게 말했다

how it had come to her. The strong man sank / trembling
그것이 어떻게 수중에 들어 오게 되었는지. 완고한 사내는 주저앉아   부들부들 떨면서

/ into a seat / and covered his face, / ashamed and almost
그 자리에   얼굴을 가렸다,   부끄러움에 두렵기까지 한 심정으로.

afraid. "I have been cruel to the lad," / he muttered at
"나는 그 녀석한테 내가 악독하게 굴었는데," 그는 마침내 중얼거렸다:

length: / "I deserved not to have good / at his hands."
"나는 도움받을 자격이 없어   그 아이에게."

Little Alois, / taking courage, / crept close to her father /
알루아는,   용기를 내서,   아버지에게 살며시 다가가

and nestled against him / her fair curly head. "Nello may
그의 곁에 기대었다   곱슬곱슬한 고운 머리를.

come here again, / father?" / she whispered. "He may
"넬로가 와도 괜찮을까요,   아빠?"   그녀가 속삭였다.   "와도 되는 거죠

come / to-morrow as he used to do?"
예전처럼?"

The miller pressed her in his arms: / his hard, sunburned
방앗간 주인은 딸을 두 팔로 꼭 끌어 안았다: 그의 냉정하고, 그을린 얼굴은

face / was very pale / and his mouth trembled. "Surely,
매우 창백해졌고   입술은 떨리고 있었다.   "그럼, 물론이지,"

surely," / he answered his child. "He shall bide here / on
그가 딸에게 대답했다.   "넬로는 여기에 머물 거야

Christmas Day, / and any other day / he will. God helping
크리스마스에,   그리고 다른 날도   그가 원한다면. 오 하나님,

me, / I will make amends to the boy / — I will make
제가,   그 소년에게 빚을 갚겠습니다   — 제가 빚을 갚겠습니다."

amends."

Little Alois kissed him / in gratitude and joy, / then slid
알루아는 아버지에게 입맞춤했다   감사하고 기쁜 마음에,   그리고는 아버지의

from his knees / and ran to where the dog / kept watch by
무릎에서 내려와   개가 있는 곳으로 달려갔다   계속 문을 바라보고 있던.

the door. "And to-night / I may feast Patrasche?" / she cried
      "그리고 오늘 밤은   파트라슈를 대접해도 되죠?"   알루아가 소리쳤다

/ in a child's thoughtless glee.
아이 특유의 철부지 같은 기쁨에 젖어.

Her father bent his head gravely: / "Ay, ay: / let the dog
그녀의 아버지는 근엄하게 고개를 끄덕였다: "당연하지: 그 개에게 제일 좋은 것을

have the best;" / for the stern old man was moved and
먹이렴:"   엄격한 노신사는 감동했기 때문이다

shaken / to his heart's depths.
마음속 깊이.

Key Expression ❢

try to와 try ~ing

동사 중에는 뒤에 to 부정사와 동명사가 올 때 의미가 달라지는 것들이 있습니다. try는 뒤에 to 부정사가 오면 '~하기 위해 노력하다', 동명사가 오면 '~하는 것을 시도하다, 시험 삼아 ~해 보다'의 의미로 해석합니다.

ex) Patrasche was trying with every art he knew to call him back to life.
파트라슈는 알고 있는 모든 방법을 동원해 그가 정신을 차리게 하려고 노력했다.
They tried all they could to solace him.
그들은 파트라슈를 달래려고 최대한 노력했다.

---

jade 물린, 실증난 | presence 존재 | ashen 잿빛인 | lantern 손전등 | maiden 아가씨 | portion 부분, 몫 | sink
가라앉다 | creep 살금살금 움직이다 | sunburned 그을린 | amend 수정하다 | thoughtless 무심한, 배려 없는

111

It was Christmas Eve, / and the mill-house was filled / with
그날은 크리스마스 이브였고,   방앗간에는 가득했다

oak logs / and squares of turf, / with cream and honey, /
참나무 장작들과 땔감들과,   크림과 꿀,

with meat and bread, / and the rafters were hung / with
고기와 빵들이,   그리고 서까래에는 걸려 있었다

wreaths of evergreen, / and the Calvary and the cuckoo
상록수로 만든 화환이,   또한 수난상과 뻐꾸기 시계는

clock / looked out from a mass of holly. There were little
        호랑가시 나무 장식 더미 중에서 도드라져 보였다.   작은 종이 등이 있었고,

paper lanterns, / too, / for Alois, / and toys of various
              또한,   알루아에게 줄,   다양한 종류의 장난감과

fashions / and sweetmeats in bright-pictured papers. There
              알록달록한 그림 종이로 싼 사탕들도 있었다.

were light and warmth and abundance / everywhere, / and
불빛과 따뜻함과 풍요로움이 있었다   어디에나,

the child would fain / have made the dog a guest honored
그리고 소녀는 기꺼이   파트라슈를 손님으로 맞아 대접했다.

and feasted.

But Patrasche / would neither lie in the warmth / nor share
하지만 파트라슈는   따뜻한 곳에 누우려 하지도 않았고   즐거움을 나누려

in the cheer. Famished he was / and very cold, / but without
하지도 않았다. 매우 굶주렸고   추웠지만,   넬로 없이는

Nello / he would partake / neither of comfort nor food.
파트라슈는 누리려 하지 않았다 편안함도 음식도.

Against all temptation / he was proof, / and close against
모든 유혹을 뿌리치고   그는 견뎌냈다,   문 근처 가까이에 서서

the door / he leaned always, / watching only for a means of
줄곧 기대어,   탈출 방법만을 찾으려 했다.

escape.

---

turf 토탄, 땔감 | rafter 서까래 | holly 호랑가시 나무, 크리스마스 장식용으로 쓰임 | sweetmeat 사탕 |
abundance 풍부 | fain 기꺼이 | famish 굶주리다 | partake 참여하다 | proof (손상 등에) 견딜 수 있는

"He wants the lad," / said Baas Cogez. "Good dog! good
"파트라슈가 그 아이를 원하는 구나," 코제 나리가 말했다.   "훌륭한 개로구나!

dog! / I will go over to the lad / the first thing at day-dawn."
좋은 개야! 내가 그 아이에게 가 봐야겠어   내일 아침이 밝자마자 바로."

113

For no one but Patrasche knew / that Nello had left the hut,
파트라슈를 외에는 누구도 알지 못했다　　넬로가 그 오두막집을 떠났다는 것을.

/ and no one but Patrasche divined / that Nello had gone /
그리고 파트라슈를 외에는 누구도 예측하지 못했다　　넬로가 가 버렸다는 것을

to face starvation and misery / alone.
굶주림과 고통에 맞서려고　　홀로.

The mill-kitchen was very warm: / great logs crackled and
방앗간의 부엌은 매우 따뜻했다:　　거대한 통나무들이 탁탁거리며 타오르고

flamed / on the hearth; / neighbors came in / for a glass
있었고　　난로 안에서;　　이웃들이 들어왔다　　와인을 한 잔 하러

of wine / and a slice of the fat goose baking / for supper.
　　거위 구이와 함께　　저녁으로.

Alois, / gleeful / and sure of her playmate back / on the
알루아는,　　기쁨에 가득 차서　자신의 친구가 돌아올 것을 의심하지 않으며

morrow, / bounded and sang / and tossed back her yellow
그 다음 날에,　　뛰어다니며 노래했다　　금발 머리를 찰랑거리며.

hair. Baas Cogez, / in the fulness of his heart, / smiled
코제 나리는,　　가슴이 벅차 올라,

on her through / moistened eyes, / and spoke of / the way
알루아에게 미소 지었고　　눈시울이 젖은 채,　　이야기 했다

in which he would befriend / her favorite companion;
도울 방법을　　딸이 가장 좋아하는 친구를;

/ the house-mother sat with calm, / contented face / at
안주인은 차분하게 앉아,　　만족스러운 얼굴로

the spinning-wheel; / the cuckoo in the clock / chirped
돌아가는 물레를 바라보았다;　시계 속 뻐꾸기는　　매 시간마다

mirthful hours. Amidst it all / Patrasche was bidden / with
유쾌하게 울어댔다.　이 모든 와중에　　파트라슈에게 쏟아졌다

a thousand words of welcome / to tarry there a cherished
천 마디의 환영의 말들이　　귀한 손님으로 머물게 된 것에.

guest. But / neither peace nor plenty / could allure him /
하지만　평안함이나 풍성함도　　파트라슈를 끌어들이지 못했다

where Nello was not.
넬로가 없는 곳에서는.

divine 예상하다 | crackle 탁탁 소리를 내다 | flame 활활 타오르다 | playmate 놀이 친구 | moisten 촉촉해지다
| spinning-wheel 물레 | chirp 짹짹 거리다 | mirthful 유쾌한 | tarry 머물다 | the Christ-child 아기 예수 |
unlatch 빗장을 끄르다 | cosey 아늑함(cozy로도 씀) | slumber 잠 | bygone 지나간, 옛날의

When the supper smoked / on the board, / and the voices /
저녁 식사가 김을 모락모락 피우고   식탁 위에서,   목소리들이

were loudest and gladdest, / and the Christ-child brought
크고 유쾌하게 울려 퍼졌으며,   아기 예수가 훌륭한 선물을 주었을 때

choicest gifts / to Alois, / Patrasche, / watching always an
좋은 선물을   알루아에게.   파트라슈는,   기회만 계속 엿보고 있다가,

occasion, / glided out / when the door was unlatched / by a
빠져 나갔다   문의 빗장이 풀렸을 때

careless new-comer, / and as swiftly / as his weak and tired
한 조심성 없는 손님에 의해,   최대한 빨리

limbs would bear him / sped over the snow / in the bitter,
허약하고 지친 다리가 견딜 수 있는 한   눈길 위에서 속도를 냈다   혹독하고 암흑같은 밤에.

black night. He had only one thought / — to follow Nello.
파트라슈에게는 한 가지 생각 뿐이었다   — 넬로를 따라 가야 한다는.

A human friend might have paused / for the pleasant meal,
사람이었다면 멈췄을지도 모른다   맛있는 음식과,

/ the cheery warmth, / the cosey slumber; / but that was
즐거운 온기와,   안락한 잠자리를 위해;

not the friendship of Patrasche. He remembered a bygone
하지만 파트라슈의 우정은 그런 것이 아니었다.   그는 지난날의 시간을 떠올렸다,

time, / when an old man and a little child had found him /
할아버지와 어린 소년이 그를 발견했을 때를

sick unto death / in the wayside ditch.
아파서 죽어가던   길가 배수로에서.

 mini test 7

A. 다음 문장을 해석해 보세요.

(1) He claimed / in default of his rent / every stick and stone, / every pot and pan, / in the hut.
→

(2) The woman shut the door hastily, / murmuring some vague saying / about wheat and rye being very dear / that season.
→

(3) When Nello recovered his consciousness / he was lying on the stones without, / and Patrasche was trying / with every art he knew / to call him back to life.
→

(4) Suddenly / Patrasche paused, / arrested by a scent in the snow, / scratched, whined, / and drew out with his teeth / a small case of brown leather.
→

B. 다음 주어진 문장이 되도록 빈칸에 써 넣으세요.

(1) 그곳에서의 삶은 고된 일과 가난으로 가득 차 있었지만, 그래도 그들은 아주 만족했다.
There life in it _____, and yet they had been so well content.

(2) 내게 뭐라도 있었으면 팔아서 파트라슈에게 빵을 사줄 수 있을 텐데!
If I had anything about me _____ !

(3) 안주인과 소녀는 기쁨과 두려움에 아무 말도 못하고 서 있었다.
The woman and the child _____ .

 Answer

A. (1) 그는 집세의 대가로 오두막에 있는 모든 나무토막과 돌멩이 하나, 모든 솥과 냄비까지 요구했다. (2) 그 집여자는 이번 겨울에는 밀과 호밀이 아주 귀하다고 애매모호하게 중얼거리며 서둘러 문을 닫았다. (3) 넬로가 다시 의식을 차렸을 때 그는 아무것도 없는 돌바닥 위에 누워 있었고, 파트라슈는 알고 있는 모든 방법을 동원하

116   *A Dog of Flanders*

(4) <u>이 개가 저를 따라 오지 못하게 막아 주세요.</u>

Keep him

C. 다음 주어진 문구가 알맞은 문장이 되도록 순서를 맞춰 보세요.

(1) 쫓겨나도록 기다리지 않을 거야. 가자.
   [will not / kicked out: / We / to / let / wait / be / go / us]
   → The rest of the great officers are

(2) 그것을 보자 넬로는 충격으로 정신이 약간 혼미해졌다.
   [his stupor / from / roused / the lad / The sight / a little]
   → He desired I would stand like a Colossus,

(3) 그들은 파트라슈를 달래보려고 최대한 노력했다.
   [him / all / tried / they / solace / They / to / could]
   → I swore and subscribed to these articles

(4) 나는 그 아이에게 도움받을 자격이 없어.
   [to / good / deserved / his hands / I / not / have / at]
   →

D. 다음 단어에 대한 맞는 설명과 연결해 보세요.

(1) shudder   ▶   ◀ ① near darkness

(2) proclaim   ▶   ◀ ② shake with fear or cold

(3) throng   ▶   ◀ ③ a large crowd of people

(4) gloom   ▶   ◀ ④ make something known to the
                          public

8

Snow had fallen freshly / all the evening long; / it was
눈이 새롭게 내렸었다   그 날 저녁 내내;

now nearly ten; / the trail of the boy's footsteps / was
이제 거의 10시가 되었다;   소년의 발자국 흔적은

almost obliterated. It took Patrasche long / to discover any
거의 없어져 버렸다.   파트라슈에겐 오랜 시간이 걸렸다   냄새를 찾아내는데.

scent. When at last he found it, / it was lost again quickly,
마침내 그 냄새를 찾았다가도,   다시 금새 사라져버렸다,

/ and lost and recovered, / and again lost and again
놓쳤다가 다시 찾고,   또 놓쳤다가 다시 찾고,

recovered, / a hundred times or more.
백 번도 더 넘게 반복했다.

The night was very wild. The lamps under the wayside
그 날 밤은 날씨가 매우 거칠었다.   길가의 십자가 아래 켜 놓은 등불은

crosses / were blown out; / the roads were sheets of ice; /
바람에 꺼져버렸고;   길은 빙판처럼 얼어 붙었으며;

the impenetrable darkness / hid every trace of habitations;
칠흑 같은 어둠이   사람이 사는 흔적을 모두 감춰 버려서;

/ there was no living thing abroad. All the cattle were
살아있는 것은 아무것도 없었다.   가축들도 모두 우리 안으로 들어갔고,

housed, / and in all the huts and homesteads / men and
모든 오두막과 농가에서는

women rejoiced and feasted. There was only Patrasche
남녀가 기뻐하며 잔치를 벌였다.   오직 파트라슈만이

/ out in the cruel cold / — old and famished / and full of
매서운 추위 속에 나와 있었다   — 늙고 굶주려서   고통스러웠지만,

pain, / but with the strength and the patience / of a great
힘을 내서 끈기 있게   위대한 사랑으로

love / to sustain him / in his search.
버텨내며   넬로를 찾았다.

---

oblterate 없애다 | blow out 불어 끄다 | impenetrable 눈 앞이 안 보이는 | habitation 주거지 | sustain
지속하다 | tortuous 꼬불꼬불한 | gleam 어슴프레 빛나다 | crevice 틈 | riot 폭동 | creak 삐걱거리다

The trail of Nello's steps, / faint and obscure / as it
넬로의 발자국의 흔적은, 희미하고 잘 보이지 않았지만

was under the new snow, / went straightly / along the
새로 쌓인 눈에 덮여서, 곧장 뻗어 있었다

accustomed tracks / into Antwerp. It was past midnight /
낯익은 길을 따라 안트베르펜으로 향하는. 자정이 넘은 시간이었다

when Patrasche traced it / over the boundaries of the town
파트라슈가 흔적을 따라간 때는 마을 어귀를 벗어나

/ and into the narrow, tortuous, gloomy streets. It was all
좁고, 구불구불한, 음산한 길로. 온통 캄캄했다

quite dark / in the town, / save where some light gleamed
마을은, 약간의 불빛이 불그스름하게 새어 나오거나

ruddily / through the crevices of house-shutters, / or some
닫힌 덧문 틈으로,

group went homeward / with lanterns / chanting drinking-
몇몇 사람들이 집으로 가면서 등불을 들고 술에 취해 노래 부르는 것 말고는.

songs. The streets were all white / with ice: / the high walls
거리는 온통 하얗게 보였고 얼음에 뒤덮여: 높은 담장이나 지붕은

and roofs / loomed black / against them. There was scarce
어렴풋이 검게 보였다 그와 대비되어. 거의 아무 소리도 없었다

a sound / save the riot of the winds / down the passages /
바람이 내는 소음을 제외하고는 길가에서

as they tossed the creaking signs / and shook the tall lamp-
간판을 때리며 삐걱거리고 높이 매달린 가로등을 흔들며 일으키는.

irons.

Key Expression ♀

'시간이 걸리다'의 take

'~가 …하는데 시간이 걸리다'라는 의미를 표현할 때는 동사 take를 사용합니다.

▶ it + take + 사람 + 시간 + to 부정사

이때, it은 시간을 나타내는 비인칭 주어입니다. 이와 같은 4형식 문장은 아래와
같이 to 부정사의 의미상 주어를 사용하여 3형식 문장으로 바꿀 수 있습니다.

▶ it + take + 시간 + for + 목적격 + to 부정사

ex) It took Patrasche long to discover any scent.
파트라슈가 어떤 냄새를 찾아내는 데에는 오랜 시간이 걸렸다.

So many passers-by had trodden / through and through the
수많은 행인들이 밟고 지나갔고   몇 번이고 눈 위를,

snow, / so many diverse paths / had crossed and recrossed
수많은 흔적들이   엇갈리고 다시 만나서

/ each other, / that the dog had a hard task / to retain any
서로서로,   파트라슈에게는 정말 힘든 일이었었다   놓치지 않고 계속 따라

hold on / the track he followed. But he kept on his way, /
가는 것이   쫓고 있는 흔적을.   하지만 파트라슈는 계속해서 길을 갔다,

though the cold pierced him / to the bone, / and the jagged
추위가 그를 파고 들었고   뼛속까지,   날카로운 얼음 조각에

ice / cut his feet, / and the hunger in his body / gnawed like
발을 베었으며,   온몸에 사무친 배고픔이   쥐의 이빨처럼 갉아

a rat's teeth. He kept on his way, / a poor gaunt, / shivering
들었지만.   파트라슈는 길을 계속 갔다,   불쌍할 정도로 비쩍 마른   부들부들 떠는

thing, / and by long patience / traced the steps he loved /
이 짐승은,   오랫동안 인내하며   사랑하는 이의 발자국을 쫓아갔고

into the very heart of the burgh / and up to the steps / of
마을의 가장 중심부에 이르렀다   그리고 계단으로 이어져 있었다

the great cathedral.
대성당의.

"He is gone to / the things that he loved," / thought
"넬로는 찾아갔구나   자신이 사랑했던 것을."   파트라슈는 생각했다:

Patrasche: / he could not understand, / but he was full of
파트라슈는 이해할 수 없었지만,   슬픔과 연민으로 가득 찼다

sorrow and of pity / for the art-passion / that to him / was
넬로의 그림에 대한 열정에   그로서는

so incomprehensible / and yet so sacred.
이해할 수 없었지만   너무나 신성한

The portals of the cathedral / were unclosed / after the
대성당의 문들은   열린 채였다

midnight mass. Some heedlessness in the custodians, / too
자정 미사가 끝난 후.   성당 관리인의 실수로 인해,

passer-by 행인 | tread 걸음을 디디다 | diverse 다양한 | recross 다시 가로지르다 | gnaw 갉아 먹다 | gaunt
수척한, 여윈 | incomprehensible 이해할 수 없는 | heedlessness 부주의함 | custodian 관리인 | thread 실
intense 극심한 | immensity 방대함 | vaulted 아치형의, 둥근 | forsake 저버리다

eager to go home / and feast or sleep, / or too drowsy / to
너무나 집에 가고 싶었거나,   축제에 가거나 자고 싶었거나,   혹은 너무 졸려서

know whether they turned the keys aright, / had left one
열쇠를 제대로 돌렸는지도 몰라서,

of the doors unlocked. By that accident / the foot-falls /
문 하나를 잠그지 않은 채 두어 버린. 그 실수로 인해   그 발자국은

Patrasche sought / had passed through / into the building,
파트라슈가 찾고 있던   들어갈 수 있었다   빌딩 안으로,

/ leaving the white marks of snow / upon the dark stone
하얀 눈 자국을 남기며   짙은 돌 바닥 위에.

floor. By that slender white thread, / frozen as it fell, / he
하얀 실낱같은 목숨을 부지한 채,   온몸이 얼어 쓰러질 듯 했지만,

was guided / through the intense silence, / through the
그는 이끌려 갔다   극심한 고요함을 지나,

immensity of the vaulted space / — guided straight / to
둥근 천장이 있는 넓은 방을 지나   — 곧장 이끌려 갔다

the gates of * the chancel, / and, / stretched there upon the
성단소의 입구까지,   그리고,   그곳 돌바닥 위에 쓰러져 있는,

stones, / he found Nello. He crept up / and touched the face
넬로를 발견했다.   파트라슈는 기어가서   소년의 얼굴을 건드렸다.

of the boy. "Didst thou dream / that I should be faithless /
"생각한 거니   내가 의리 없이

and forsake thee? I — a dog?" / said that / mute caress.
널 저버릴 거라고?   내가 — 한 마리 개가?" 그렇게 말했다   말없는 몸짓은.

Key Expression ♥

'형용사 + as + 주어 + 동사'의 양보구문

'형용사 + as[though] + 주어 + 동사'의 형태는 '~라고 하더라도, ~했지만'라는 의미의 양보구문이에요.
형용사 자리에는 부사, 명사, 동사원형이 들어가기도 하며 명사의 경우 관사 없이 사용합니다. 또한 as 대신에 though를 사용하기도 합니다.

ex) Frozen as it fell, he was guided straight to the gates of the chancel.
꽁꽁 얼어 쓰러질 것 같았지만, 그는 성단소의 입구까지 곧장 이끌려 들어갔다.

---

* 성단소 : 성당에서 성가대와 성직자가 위치하는 자리

121

The lad raised himself / with a low cry / and clasped him
소년은 몸을 일으켜 세우고   낮은 신음 소리를 내며   파트라슈를 꼭 끌어 안았다.

close. "Let us lie down / and die together," / he murmured.
"여기에 눕자   그리고 같이 죽는 거야."   넬로가 속삭였다.

"Men have no need of us, / and we are all alone."
"사람들은 우리가 필요 없어,   그리고 우리는 외톨이니까."

In answer, / Patrasche crept closer yet, / and laid his head /
대답 대신,   파트라슈는 더욱 가까이 몸을 붙이며,   머리를 뉘었다

upon the young boy's breast. The great tears stood / in his
어린 소년의 가슴 위에.   커다란 눈물 방울이 맺혔다

brown, sad eyes: / not for himself / — for himself / he was
그의 서글픈 갈색 눈에: 자신을 위해서가 아니었다   — 오히려 자신은

happy.
행복했으니까.

They lay close together / in the piercing cold. The blasts /
둘은 꼭 붙어서 누웠다   살을 에는 추위 속에서.   거센 바람이

that blew over the Flemish dikes / from the northern seas
플란다스의 둑을 넘어서 불어온   북쪽 바다로부터

/ were like waves of ice, / which froze every living thing /
얼음의 파도와 같아서,   살아있는 모든 것을 얼려버렸다

they touched. The interior of the immense vault of stone /
건드리는 것마다.   거대한 둥근 천장의 건물 안에는

in which they were / was even more bitterly chill / than the
그들이 있던   더욱 매서운 한기가 돌았다

Key Expression ♟

lie와 lay의 구별

lie와 lay는 혼동하기 쉬운 동사들입니다. lie는 자동사로 뒤에 목적어가 오지 않으며, lay는 타동사이므로 뒤에 목적어가 따라 온다는 사실을 기억하세요. 과거형 변화에서 겹치는 단어도 있으므로 같이 기억해 두세요.

▶lie : (자동사) 눕다, 놓여 있다 ⇒ lie-lay-lain
▶lay : (타동사) 눕히다, 놓다 ⇒ lay-laid-laid

ex) They lay close together in the piercing cold. (lie의 과거형)
    그들은 살을 에는 추위 속에 함께 누웠다.
    Patrasche crept closer yet, and laid his head upon the young boy's breast.
    (lay의 과거형)
    파트라슈는 더 가까이 기어가, 머리를 소년의 가슴 위에 놓았다.

snow-covered plains without. Now and then / a bat moved
아무것도 없는 눈 덮인 들판보다도.　　　　　　이따금씩　　　　　박쥐가 날아다녔다

in the shadows / — now and then / a gleam of light came /
어둠 속에서　　— 또 이따금씩　　희미한 불빛이 어른거렸다

on the ranks of carven figures. Under the Rubens / they lay
죽 늘어선 조각상에.　　　　　루벤스의 그림 아래　　그들은 같이

together / quite still, / and soothed almost into a dreaming
누워서　　꼼짝 않고,　　거의 꿈 속으로 가라앉았다

slumber / by the numbing narcotic of the cold. Together /
추위라는 진정제에 온몸이 마비되어서.　　　　　　함께

they dreamed of / the old glad days / when they had chased
둘은 오래 전 행복했던 날에 대해 꿈을 꾸었다　　서로를 좇아다니던 때를

each other / through the flowering grasses / of the summer
　　　　꽃 핀 풀밭 사이로　　　　여름날의 초원의,

meadows, / or sat hidden / in the tall bulrushes / by the
　　　혹은 숨어 앉아서　　키 큰 골풀 속에

water's side, / watching / the boats go seaward / in the sun.
물가에 있는,　　바라보았던 때를　　배들이 바다로 떠나는 모습을　　태양 아래에서.

Suddenly / through the darkness / a great white radiance
갑자기　　어둠을 뚫고　　　　거대한 하얀 빛줄기가 흘러 들어왔다

streamed / through the vastness of the aisles; / the moon, /
　　　넓은 복도를 통과하여;　　　　　　　달이,

that was at her height, / had broken through the clouds, / the
높이 떠서,　　　　구름을 뚫고 빛을 비췄고,

snow had ceased to fall, / the light reflected from the snow
눈이 그쳐서,　　　　쌓인 눈에 반사된 달빛은

without / was clear as the light of dawn. It fell through the
　　새벽녘 햇살만큼이나 선명했다.　　　빛은 둥근 천장을 통과해서

arches full / upon the two pictures above, / from which the
가득 비췄다　　두 점의 그림 위를,

boy on his entrance / had flung back the veil: / the Elevation
소년이 들어오는 길에　　그림을 가린 장막을 걷어 버린 것이었다: '십자가에 들어 올려지는

and the Descent of the Cross / were for one instant visible.
그리스도'와 '십자가에서 내려지는 그리스도'가　　한 순간에 눈에 들어왔다.

---

dike 둑, 제방 | rank 나란히 세우다 | narcotic 진정제, 수면제 | radiance 빛, 광채 | reflect 비추다, 반사하다

Nello rose to his feet / and stretched his arms to them; /
넬로는 일어서서　　　　　그림을 향해 두 팔을 뻗었다;

the tears of a passionate ecstasy / glistened on the paleness
열정적인 환희의 눈물이　　　　　그의 창백한 얼굴 위에서 반짝였다.

of his face. "I have seen them at last!" / he cried aloud. "O
"마침내 그림들을 봤어!"　　　　　그는 큰 소리로 외쳤다.

God, / it is enough!"
"오 하나님, 이제 됐습니다!"

His limbs failed under him, / and he sank upon his knees,
팔다리에 힘이 풀려서,　　　　　그는 무릎을 꿇고 주저 앉았지만,

/ still gazing upward / at the majesty / that he adored. For a
여전히 우러러 보고 있었다　　그 위대한 작품을　　그가 동경하는.

few brief moments / the light illumined the divine visions /
얼마 안 되는 짧은 순간 동안　　빛이 신성한 그림을 비췄다

that had been denied to him / so long / — light / clear and
그가 볼 수 없었던　　　　　그렇게 오랫동안 — 빛이

sweet and strong / as though it streamed / from the throne
선명하고 부드럽고, 강력한　　흘러내린 듯이　　　하늘의 권좌로부터 내려온 듯.

of Heaven. Then suddenly / it passed away: / once more / a
그러더니 갑자기　　빛이 사라져 버렸고;　　다시 한 번

great darkness covered / the face of Christ.
막막한 어둠이 뒤덮어 버렸다　　그리스도의 얼굴을.

The arms of the boy / drew close again / the body of the
소년의 팔은　　　　　다시 끌어 안았다　　개의 몸뚱이를.

dog. "We shall see His face / — there," / he murmured; /
"그분의 얼굴을 보게 될 거야　　— 그곳에서,"　넬로가 웅얼거렸다;

"and He will not part us, / I think."
"그리고 그분은 우리를 갈라놓지 않으실 거야, 내 생각에는."

On the morrow, / by the chancel of the cathedral, / the
다음 날,　　　　　대성당의 성단소 곁에서,

people of Antwerp found them both. They were both dead:
안트베르펜의 사람들이 그 둘을 발견했다.　　　그 둘 다 숨이 멎어 있었다:

/ the cold of the night / had frozen into stillness / alike
밤의 추위가　　　　　꽁꽁 얼려 버린 것이었다

the young life and the old. When the Christmas morning
어린 소년과 늙은 개의 생명을 모두.　　크리스마스의 아침이 밝았고

broke / and the priests came to the temple, / they saw / them
신부들이 성당 안으로 들어왔을 때,   그들은 보았다   그들이

lying thus / on the stones together. Above / the veils were
그렇게 누워 있는 것을 그렇게 돌바닥 위에 함께.   위쪽에는   장막이 벗겨져 있었다

drawn back / from the great visions of Rubens, / and the
루벤스의 위대한 작품을 가렸던,

fresh rays of the sunrise / touched / the thorn-crowned head
떠오르는 태양의 생생한 빛줄기가   어루만지고 있었다 가시면류관을 쓴 그리스도의 머리를.

of the Christ.

As the day grew on / there came an old, / hard-featured
아침이 지나자   그곳에 한 노인이 찾아왔다,   고집스럽게 생긴 남자가

man / who wept as women weep. "I was cruel to the lad,"
여자들처럼 훌쩍훌쩍 우는.   "내가 이 아이에게 무자비했어요,"

/ he muttered, / "and now I would have made amends / —
그는 중얼거렸다,   "이제 보상을 하겠습니다   — 네,

yea, / to the half of my substance / — and he should have
그렇습니다, 내 재산의 반을 내놓겠어요   — 그는 되었어야 했는데."

been / to me / as a son."
내게   아들같은 존재로

There came also, / as the day grew apace, / a painter /
그곳에 또 다른 사람이 왔다,   시간이 지난 후,   화가였다

who had fame in the world, / and who was liberal of hand
세상에 명성이 자자한,   씀씀이도 마음씨도 후하다고 알려진.

*공현 축일. 동방 박사 삼 인이 예수를 찾은 날. 예수가 태어난 지 12번째 되는 날인 1월 6일이다. 서양의
가톨릭 전통에서는 이날도 크리스마스에 버금가는 명절이다.

and of spirit. "I seek one / who should have had the prize /
"한 사람을 찾습니다   그 상을 받았어야 마땅했던

yesterday / had worth won," / he said to the people / — "a
어제   그리고 상을 받을 자격이 있는,"   그는 사람들에게 말했다

boy of rare promise and genius. An old wood-cutter / on a
— "보기 드문 장래성과 천재성을 지닌 아이예요.   늙은 나무꾼   쓰러진

fallen tree / at eventide / — that was all his theme. But there
나무에 앉은   황혼 무렵에   — 그게 그림의 전부였습니다.   하지만 위대함

was greatness / for the future / in it. I would fain find him, /
이 있었어요   미래에 꽃 피울   그 안에는. 나는 기꺼이 그 아이를 찾아,

and take him with me / and teach him Art."
데려가서   그림을 가르칠 것입니다."

And a little child / with curling fair hair, / sobbing bitterly
그리고 한 아이가   금발의 곱슬 머리를 한,   비통하게 흐느껴 울면서

/ as she clung to her father's arm, / cried aloud, "Oh, Nello,
그녀의 아버지의 팔에 매달려서,   크게 소리쳤다,   "넬로, 돌아와!

come! We have all ready / for thee. The Christ-child's hands
모든 것을 준비 했단 말이야   널 위해.   아기 예수의 손에는

/ are full of gifts, / and the old piper will play / for us; / and
선물이 가득하고,   피리 부는 노인이 연주해 줄 거야   우리를 위해서;

the mother says / thou shalt stay by the hearth / and burn
그리고 어머니가 말했어   난롯가에 앉아서   구운 밤을 먹자고

nuts / with us / all the Noël week long / — yes, even to *the
우리랑 함께   크리스마스 주간 내내   — 그래, 공현 축일까지 계속 말

Feast of the Kings! And Patrasche will be so happy! Oh,
이야!   그러면 파트라슈도 행복해 할 거야!

Nello, / wake and come!"
오, 넬로야,   정신 차리고 일어나 봐!"

But the young pale face, / turned upward / to the light / of
하지만 소년의 창백한 얼굴은,   고개를 들면서   빛을 향해

the great Rubens / with a smile upon its mouth, / answered
루벤스의 걸작들에 비추이는   입술에 미소를 머금고,   모두에게 대답했다,

them all, / "It is too late."
"너무 늦었어요."

substance 물질 | apace 빠른 속도로 | fame 명성 | liberal 진보적인 | promise 장래성, 가능성 | eventide
저녁, 밤 | piper 피리 부는 사람

For the sweet, sonorous bells / went ringing / through the
감미롭고, 낭랑한 종소리가   울려 퍼졌고   추위를 뚫고,

frost, / and the sunlight shone / upon the plains of snow,
햇살이 빛났다   눈 덮인 들판 위에서,

/ and the populace trooped / gay and glad / through the
그리고 사람들은 무리 지어 걸어갔다   명랑하고 기쁘게   길거리를,

streets, / but Nello and Patrasche / no more asked charity
하지만 넬로와 파트라슈는   더 이상 자비를 구걸하지 않았다

/ at their hands. All they needed / now / Antwerp gave /
사람들에게.   그들에게 필요한 것은   이제   안트베르펜이 모두 주었다

unbidden.
청하지도 않았는데.

Death had been more pitiful / to them / than longer life /
죽음은 차라리 동정이라 할 수 있었다   그들에게는   더 이상 삶에서

would have been. It had taken / the one / in the loyalty of
받을 수 있는 것보다.   죽음은 데려갔다   한 생명과   충직한 사랑을 품었던,

love, / and the other / in the innocence of faith, / from a
또 다른 생명을   순진무구한 믿음을 가졌던,   이 세상으로부터

world / which for love / has no recompense / and for faith /
그 사랑에   아무 보상도 받지 못하고

no fulfilment.
믿음 또한 이뤄지지 못한.

All their lives / they had been together, / and in their
그들이 살아온 평생동안 둘은 함께였고,   죽음에 있어서도

deaths / they were not divided: / for when they were found
둘은 헤어지지 않았다: 왜냐하면 그들이 발견되었을 때

/ the arms of the boy were folded too closely / around the
소년의 팔이 너무 꼭 안고 있어서   개를 감싸고

dog / to be severed / without violence, / and the people of
떼어놓을 수 없었다   무력을 사용하지 않고는,   그래서 마을 사람들은,

their little village, / contrite and ashamed, / implored a
잘못을 뉘우치고 부끄러워하며,

---

populace 대중 | recompense 보상 | contrite 깊이 뉘우치는 | implore 애원하다

special grace / for them, / and, / making them one grave, /
특별한 은총을 기원했다 그들을 위해, 그리고, 그들에게 하나의 무덤을 만들어,

laid them to rest there / side by side / — forever!
그곳에서 쉴 수 있도록 안치했다 나란히 — 영원토록!

 mini test 8

A. 다음 문장을 해석해 보세요.

(1) It was all quite dark / in the town, / save where some light gleamed ruddily / through the crevices of house-shutters, / or some group went homeward with lanterns / chanting drinkingsongs.
→

(2) So many passers-by had trodden / through and through the snow, / so many diverse paths had crossed and recrossed / each other, / that the dog had a hard task / to retain any hold on / the track he followed.
→

(3) I would have made amends - yea, / to the half of my substance.
→

(4) Nello and Patrasche / no more asked charity / at their hands.
→

B. 다음 주어진 문구가 알맞은 문장이 되도록 순서를 맞춰 보세요.

(1) 파트라슈가 냄새를 찾아내는 데에는 오랜 시간이 걸렸다.
(Patrasche / took / It / any scent / to discover / long)
→

(2) 온몸이 얼어붙어 쓰러질 듯 했지만, 그는 성단소의 입구까지 곧장 이끌려 갔다.
(it / Frozen / fell / as)

_____, he was guided straight to the gates of the chancel.

(3) 어제 그 상을 받았어야 마땅했던 한 사람을 찾습니다.
(have / who / one / should / had / yesterday / the prize)
I seek _____.

 Answer

A. (1) 닫힌 덧문 틈으로 불빛이 불그스름하게 새어 나오거나 등불을 들고 집으로 향하는 몇몇 사람들이 술에 취해 노래 부르는 것을 제외하면 마을은 온통 깜깜했다. (2) 수많은 행인들이 눈 위를 여러 번 밟고 지나가서, 수많은 방향의 흔적이 엇갈리고 다시 만났기 때문에 파트라슈는 쫓고 있는 흔적을 놓치지 않고

(4) 소년의 팔이 개를 감싼 채 너무 꼭 안고 있어서 무력을 사용하지 않고는 떼어
놓을 수 없었다.
(closely / too / around / violence / the dog / to / without / be
severed)

The arms of the boy were folded
_____ .

C. 다음 주어진 문장이 본문의 내용과 맞으면 T, 틀리면 F에 동그라미 하세요.

(1) Nello disappeared with Patrasche.
(T / F)

(2) Alois' father allow Nello to stay at his house.
(T / F)

(3) Patrasche had difficulties in discovering Nello's trace.
(T / F)

(4) Nello's and Patrasche finally died together.
(T / F)

D. 의미가 비슷한 것끼리 서로 연결해 보세요.

(1) gleam ▶   ◀ ① appear

(2) loom ▶   ◀ ② blow

(3) blast ▶   ◀ ③ willingly

(4) fain ▶   ◀ ④ glisten

A Dog of Flanders를 다시 읽어 보세요.

1

Nello and Patrasche were left all alone in the world.

They were friends in a friendship closer than brotherhood. Nello
was a little Ardennois — Patrasche was a big Fleming. They were
both of the same age by length of years, yet one was still young, and
the other was already old. They had dwelt together almost all their
days: both were orphaned and destitute, and owed their lives to the
same hand. It had been the beginning of the tie between them, their
first bond of sympathy; and it had strengthened day by day, and had
grown with their growth, firm and indissoluble, until they loved one
another very greatly. Their home was a little hut on the edge of a
little village — a Flemish village a league from Antwerp, set amidst
flat breadths of pasture and corn-lands, with long lines of poplars
and of alders bending in the breeze on the edge of the great canal
which ran through it. It had about a score of houses and homesteads,
with shutters of bright green or sky-blue, and roofs rose-red or black
and white, and walls white-washed until they shone in the sun like
snow. In the centre of the village stood a windmill, placed on a little
moss-grown slope: it was a landmark to all the level country round.
It had once been painted scarlet, sails and all, but that had been in
its infancy, half a century or more earlier, when it had ground wheat
for the soldiers of Napoleon; and it was now a ruddy brown, tanned
by wind and weather. It went queerly by fits and starts, as though
rheumatic and stiff in the joints from age, but it served the whole
neighborhood, which would have thought it almost as impious to
carry grain elsewhere as to attend any other religious service than
the mass that was performed at the altar of the little old gray church,
with its conical steeple, which stood opposite to it, and whose single

bell rang morning, noon, and night with that strange, subdued, hollow sadness which every bell that hangs in the Low Countries seems to gain as an integral part of its melody.

Within sound of the little melancholy clock almost from their birth upward, they had dwelt together, Nello and Patrasche, in the little hut on the edge of the village, with the cathedral spire of Antwerp rising in the north-east, beyond the great green plain of seeding grass and spreading corn that stretched away from them like a tideless, changeless sea. It was the hut of a very old man, of a very poor man — of old Jehan Daas, who in his time had been a soldier, and who remembered the wars that had trampled the country as oxen tread down the furrows, and who had brought from his service nothing except a wound, which had made him a cripple.

When old Jehan Daas had reached his full eighty, his daughter had died in the Ardennes, hard by Stavelot, and had left him in legacy her two-year-old son. The old man could ill contrive to support himself, but he took up the additional burden uncomplainingly, and it soon became welcome and precious to him. Little Nello — which was but a pet diminutive for Nicolas — throve with him, and the old man and the little child lived in the poor little hut contentedly. It was a very humble little mud-hut indeed, but it was clean and white as a sea-shell, and stood in a small plot of garden-ground that yielded beans and herbs and pumpkins. They were very poor, terribly poor — many a day they had nothing at all to eat. They never by any chance had enough: to have had enough to eat would have been to have reached paradise at once.

But the old man was very gentle and good to the boy, and the boy was a beautiful, innocent, truthful, tender-hearted creature; and they were happy on a crust and a few leaves of cabbage, and asked no more of earth or heaven; save indeed that Patrasche should be always with them, since without Patrasche where would they have been?

For Patrasche was their alpha and omega; their treasury and granary; their store of gold and wand of wealth; their bread-winner and minister; their only friend and comforter. Patrasche dead or gone from them, they must have laid themselves down and died likewise. Patrasche was body, brains, hands, head, and feet to both of them: Patrasche was their very life, their very soul. For Jehan Daas was old and a cripple, and Nello was but a child; and Patrasche was their dog.

A dog of Flanders — yellow of hide, large of head and limb, with wolf-like ears that stood erect, and legs bowed and feet widened in the muscular development wrought in his breed by many generations of hard service.

Patrasche came of a race which had toiled hard and cruelly from sire to son in Flanders many a century — slaves of slaves, dogs of the people, beasts of the shafts and the harness, creatures that lived straining their sinews in the gall of the cart, and died breaking their hearts on the flints of the streets.

Patrasche had been born of parents who had labored hard all their days over the sharp-set stones of the various cities and the long, shadowless, weary roads of the two Flanders and of Brabant. He had been born to no other heritage than those of pain and of toil. He had been fed on curses and baptized with blows. Why not? It was a Christian country, and Patrasche was but a dog. Before he was fully grown he had known the bitter gall of the cart and the collar. Before he had entered his thirteenth month he had become the property of a hardware-dealer, who was accustomed to wander over the land

north and south, from the blue sea to the green mountains. They
sold him for a small price, because he was so young.

This man was a drunkard and a brute. The life of Patrasche was
a life of hell. To deal the tortures of hell on the animal creation is
a way which the Christians have of showing their belief in it. His
purchaser was a sullen, ill-living, brutal Brabantois, who heaped
his cart full with pots and pans and flagons and buckets, and other
wares of crockery and brass and tin, and left Patrasche to draw the
load as best he might, whilst he himself lounged idly by the side in
fat and sluggish ease, smoking his black pipe and stopping at every
wineshop or café on the road.

Happily for Patrasche — or unhappily — he was very strong: he
came of an iron race, long born and bred to such cruel travail; so
that he did not die, but managed to drag on a wretched existence
under the brutal burdens, the scarifying lashes, the hunger, the
thirst, the blows, the curses, and the exhaustion which are the only
wages with which the Flemings repay the most patient and laborious
of all their four-footed victims. One day, after two years of this long
and deadly agony, Patrasche was going on as usual along one of the
straight, dusty, unlovely roads that lead to the city of Rubens. It was
full midsummer, and very warm. His cart was very heavy, piled
high with goods in metal and in earthenware. His owner sauntered
on without noticing him otherwise than by the crack of the whip
as it curled round his quivering loins. The Brabantois had paused
to drink beer himself at every wayside house, but he had forbidden
Patrasche to stop a moment for a draught from the canal. Going
along thus, in the full sun, on a scorching highway, having eaten
nothing for twenty-four hours, and, which was far worse to him, not
having tasted water for near twelve, being blind with dust, sore with

blows, and stupefied with the merciless weight which dragged upon his loins, Patrasche staggered and foamed a little at the mouth, and fell.

He fell in the middle of the white, dusty road, in the full glare of the sun; he was sick unto death, and motionless. His master gave him the only medicine in his pharmacy — kicks and oaths and blows with a cudgel of oak, which had been often the only food and drink, the only wage and reward, ever offered to him. But Patrasche was beyond the reach of any torture or of any curses. Patrasche lay, dead to all appearances, down in the white powder of the summer dust. After a while, finding it useless to assail his ribs with punishment and his ears with maledictions, the Brabantois — deeming life gone in him, or going so nearly that his carcass was forever useless, unless indeed someone should strip it of the skin for gloves — cursed him fiercely in farewell, struck off the leathern bands of the harness, kicked his body aside into the grass, and, groaning and muttering in savage wrath, pushed the cart lazily along the road up-hill, and left the dying dog for the ants to sting and for the crows to pick.

It was the last day before Kermesse away at Louvain, and the Brabantois was in haste to reach the fair and get a good place for his truck of brass wares. He was in fierce wrath, because Patrasche had been a strong and much-enduring animal, and because he himself had now the hard task of pushing his charette all the way to Louvain. But to stay to look after Patrasche never entered his thoughts: the beast was dying and useless, and he would steal, to replace him, the first large dog that he found wandering alone out of sight of its master. Patrasche had cost him nothing, or next to nothing, and for two long, cruel years had made him toil ceaselessly in his service from sunrise to sunset, through summer and winter, in fair weather and foul.

He had got a fair use and a good profit out of Patrasche: being human, he was wise, and left the dog to draw his last breath alone in the ditch, and have his bloodshot eyes plucked out as they might be by the birds, whilst he himself went on his way to beg and to steal, to eat and to drink, to dance and to sing, in the mirth at Louvain. A dying dog, a dog of the cart — why should he waste hours over its agonies at peril of losing a handful of copper coins, at peril of a shout of laughter?

Patrasche lay there, flung in the grass-green ditch. It was a busy road that day, and hundreds of people, on foot and on mules, in wagons or in carts, went by, tramping quickly and joyously on to Louvain. Some saw him, most did not even look: all passed on. A dead dog more or less — it was nothing in Brabant: it would be nothing anywhere in the world.

 2

After a time, among the holiday-makers, there came a little old man who was bent and lame, and very feeble. He was in no guise for feasting: he was very poorly and miserably clad, and he dragged his silent way slowly through the dust among the pleasure-seekers. He looked at Patrasche, paused, wondered, turned aside, then kneeled down in the rank grass and weeds of the ditch, and surveyed the dog with kindly eyes of pity. There was with him a little rosy, fair-haired, dark-eyed child of a few years old, who pattered in amidst the bushes, for him breast-high, and stood gazing with a pretty seriousness upon the poor, great, quiet beast.

Thus it was that these two first met — the little Nello and the big Patrasche.

The upshot of that day was, that old Jehan Daas, with much laborious effort, drew the sufferer homeward to his own little hut, which was a stone's throw off amidst the fields, and there tended him with so much care that the sickness, which had been a brain seizure, brought on by heat and thirst and exhaustion, with time and shade and rest passed away, and health and strength returned, and Patrasche staggered up again upon his four stout, tawny legs.

Now for many weeks he had been useless, powerless, sore, near to death; but all this time he had heard no rough word, had felt no harsh touch, but only the pitying murmurs of the child's voice and the soothing caress of the old man's hand.

In his sickness they too had grown to care for him, this lonely man and the little happy child. He had a corner of the hut, with a heap of dry grass for his bed; and they had learned to listen eagerly for his breathing in the dark night, to tell them that he lived; and when he first was well enough to essay a loud, hollow, broken bay, they laughed aloud, and almost wept together for joy at such a sign of his sure restoration; and little Nello, in delighted glee, hung round his rugged neck with chains of marguerites, and kissed him with fresh and ruddy lips.

So then, when Patrasche arose, himself again, strong, big, gaunt, powerful, his great wistful eyes had a gentle astonishment in them that there were no curses to rouse him and no blows to drive him; and his heart awakened to a mighty love, which never wavered once in its fidelity whilst life abode with him.

But Patrasche, being a dog, was grateful. Patrasche lay pondering long with grave, tender, musing brown eyes, watching the movements of his friends.

Now, the old soldier, Jehan Daas, could do nothing for his living but limp about a little with a small cart, with which he carried daily the milk-cans of those happier neighbors who owned cattle away into the town of Antwerp. The villagers gave him the employment a little out of charity — more because it suited them well to send their milk into the town by so honest a carrier, and bide at home themselves to look after their gardens, their cows, their poultry, or their little fields. But it was becoming hard work for the old man. He was eighty-three, and Antwerp was a good league off, or more. Patrasche watched the milk-cans come and go that one day when he had got well and was lying in the sun with the wreath of marguerites round his tawny neck.

The next morning, Patrasche, before the old man had touched the cart, arose and walked to it and placed himself betwixt its handles, and testified as plainly as dumb show could do his desire and his ability to work in return for the bread of charity that he had eaten. Jehan Daas resisted long, for the old man was one of those who thought it a foul shame to bind dogs to labor for which Nature never formed them. But Patrasche would not be gainsaid: finding they did not harness him, he tried to draw the cart onward with his teeth. At length Jehan Daas gave way, vanquished by the persistence and the gratitude of this creature whom he had succored. He fashioned his cart so that Patrasche could run in it, and this he did every morning of his life thenceforward.

When the winter came, Jehan Daas thanked the blessed fortune that had brought him to the dying dog in the ditch that fair-day of

Louvain; for he was very old, and he grew feebler with each year, and he would ill have known how to pull his load of milk-cans over the snows and through the deep ruts in the mud if it had not been for the strength and the industry of the animal he had befriended. As for Patrasche, it seemed heaven to him. After the frightful burdens that his old master had compelled him to strain under, at the call of the whip at every step, it seemed nothing to him but amusement to step out with this little light green cart, with its bright brass cans, by the side of the gentle old man who always paid him with a tender caress and with a kindly word. Besides, his work was over by three or four in the day, and after that time he was free to do as he would — to stretch himself, to sleep in the sun, to wander in the fields, to romp with the young child, or to play with his fellow-dogs. Patrasche was very happy.

Fortunately for his peace, his former owner was killed in a drunken brawl at the Kermesse of Mechlin, and so sought not after him nor disturbed him in his new and well-loved home.

A few years later, old Jehan Daas, who had always been a cripple, became so paralyzed with rheumatism that it was impossible for him to go out with the cart any more. Then little Nello, being now grown to his sixth year of age, and knowing the town well from having accompanied his grandfather so many times, took his place beside the cart, and sold the milk and received the coins in exchange, and brought them back to their respective owners with a pretty grace and seriousness which charmed all who beheld him. The little Ardennois was a beautiful child, with dark, grave, tender eyes, and a lovely bloom upon his face, and fair locks that clustered to his throat; and many an artist sketched the group as it went by him — the green cart with the brass flagons of Teniers and Mieris and Van Tal, and the great tawny-colored, massive dog, with his belled harness that chimed cheerily as he went, and the small figure that ran beside him which had little white feet in great wooden shoes, and a soft, grave, innocent, happy face like the little fair children of Rubens.

Nello and Patrasche did the work so well and so joyfully together that Jehan Daas himself, when the summer came and he was better again, had no need to stir out, but could sit in the doorway in the sun and see them go forth through the garden wicket, and then doze and dream and pray a little, and then awake again as the clock tolled three and watch for their return. And on their return Patrasche would shake himself free of his harness with a bay of glee, and Nello would recount with pride the doings of the day; and they would all go in together to their meal of rye bread and milk or soup, and would see the shadows lengthen over the great plain, and see the twilight veil the fair cathedral spire; and then lie down together to sleep peacefully while the old man said a prayer. So the days and the years went on, and the lives of Nello and Patrasche were happy, innocent, and healthful. In the spring and summer especially were they glad. Flanders is not a lovely land, and around the burgh of Rubens it is perhaps least lovely of all. Corn and colza, pasture and plough, succeed each other on the characterless plain in wearying repetition, and save by some gaunt gray tower, with its peal of pathetic bells, or some figure coming athwart the fields, made picturesque by a gleaner's bundle or a woodman's fagot, there is no change, no variety, no beauty anywhere; and he who has dwelt upon the mountains or amidst the forests feels oppressed as by imprisonment with the tedium and the endlessness of that vast and dreary level. But it is green and very fertile, and it has wide horizons that have a certain charm of their own even in their dulness and monotony; and among the rushes by the water-side the flowers grow, and the trees rise tall and fresh where the barges glide with their great hulks black against the sun, and their little green barrels and vari-colored flags gay against the leaves. Anyway, there is greenery and breadth of space enough to be as good as beauty to a child and a dog; and these two asked no better, when their work was done, than to lie buried in the lush grasses on the side of the canal, and watch the cumbrous vessels drifting by and bring the crisp salt smell of the sea among the blossoming scents of the country summer.

True, in the winter it was harder, and they had to rise in the darkness and the bitter cold, and they had seldom as much as they could have eaten any day, and the hut was scarce better than a shed when the nights were cold, although it looked so pretty in warm weather, buried in a great kindly clambering vine, that never bore fruit, indeed, but which covered it with luxuriant green tracery all through the months of blossom and harvest. In winter the winds found many holes in the walls of the poor little hut, and the vine was black and leafless, and the bare lands looked very bleak and drear without, and sometimes within the floor was flooded and then frozen. In winter it was hard, and the snow numbed the little white limbs of Nello, and the icicles cut the brave, untiring feet of Patrasche.

But even then they were never heard to lament, either of them. The child's wooden shoes and the dog's four legs would trot manfully together over the frozen fields to the chime of the bells on the harness; and then sometimes, in the streets of Antwerp, some housewife would bring them a bowl of soup and a handful of bread, or some kindly trader would throw some billets of fuel into the little cart as it went homeward, or some woman in their own village would bid them keep a share of the milk they carried for their own food; and they would run over the white lands, through the early darkness, bright and happy, and burst with a shout of joy into their home.

3

So, on the whole, it was well with them, very well; and Patrasche, meeting on the highway or in the public streets the many dogs who toiled from daybreak into nightfall, paid only with blows and curses, and loosened from the shafts with a kick to starve and freeze as best they might — Patrasche in his heart was very grateful to his fate, and thought it the fairest and the kindliest the world could hold. Though he was often very hungry indeed when he lay down at night; though he had to work in the heats of summer noons and the rasping chills of winter dawns; though his feet were often tender with wounds from the sharp edges of the jagged pavement; though he had to perform tasks beyond his strength and against his nature — yet he was grateful and content: he did his duty with each day, and the eyes that he loved smiled down on him. It was sufficient for Patrasche.

There was only one thing which caused Patrasche any uneasiness in his life, and it was this. Antwerp, as all the world knows, is full at every turn of old piles of stones, dark and ancient and majestic, standing in crooked courts, jammed against gateways and taverns, rising by the water's edge, with bells ringing above them in the air, and ever and again out of their arched doors a swell of music pealing. There they remain, the grand old sanctuaries of the past, shut in amidst the squalor, the hurry, the crowds, the unloveliness, and the commerce of the modern world, and all day long the clouds drift and the birds circle and the winds sigh around them, and beneath the earth at their feet there sleeps — RUBENS.

And the greatness of the mighty Master still rests upon Antwerp, and wherever we turn in its narrow streets his glory lies therein, so that all mean things are thereby transfigured; and as we pace slowly through the winding ways, and by the edge of the stagnant water, and through the noisome courts, his spirit abides with us, and the heroic beauty of his visions is about us, and the stones that once felt his footsteps and bore his shadow seem to arise and speak of him with living voices. For the city which is the tomb of Rubens still lives to us through him, and him alone.

It is so quiet there by that great white sepulchre — so quiet, save only when the organ peals and the choir cries aloud the Salve Regina or the Kyrie Eleison. Sure no artist ever had a greater gravestone than that pure marble sanctuary gives to him in the heart of his birthplace in the chancel of St. Jacques.

Without Rubens, what were Antwerp? A dirty, dusky, bustling mart, which no man would ever care to look upon save the traders who do business on its wharves. With Rubens, to the whole world of men it is a sacred name, a sacred soil, a Bethlehem where a god of Art saw light, a Golgotha where a god of Art lies dead.

O nations! Closely should you treasure your great men, for by them alone will the future know of you. Flanders in her generations has been wise. In his life she glorified this greatest of her sons, and in his death she magnifies his name. But her wisdom is very rare. Now, the trouble of Patrasche was this. Into these great, sad piles of stones, that reared their melancholy majesty above the crowded roofs, the child Nello would many and many a time enter, and disappear through their dark arched portals, whilst Patrasche, left without upon the pavement, would wearily and vainly ponder on what could be the charm which thus allured from him his inseparable and beloved companion. Once or twice he did essay to see for himself, clattering up the steps with his milk-cart behind him; but thereon he had been always sent back again summarily by a tall custodian in black clothes and silver chains of office; and fearful of bringing his little master into trouble, he desisted, and remained couched patiently before the churches until such time as the boy reappeared. It was not the fact of his going into them which disturbed Patrasche: he knew that people went to church: all the village went to the small, tumbledown, gray pile opposite the red windmill.

What troubled him was that little Nello always looked strangely when he came out, always very flushed or very pale; and whenever he returned home after such visitations would sit silent and dreaming, not caring to play, but gazing out at the evening skies beyond the line of the canal, very subdued and almost sad.

What was it? wondered Patrasche. He thought it could not be good or natural for the little lad to be so grave, and in his dumb fashion he tried all he could to keep Nello by him in the sunny fields or in the busy market-place. But to the churches Nello would go: most often of all would he go to the great cathedral; and Patrasche, left without on the stones by the iron fragments of Quentin Matsys's gate, would stretch himself and yawn and sigh, and even howl now and then, all in vain, until the doors closed and the child perforce came forth again, and winding his arms about the dog's neck would kiss him on his broad, tawney-colored forehead, and murmur always the same words: "If I could only see them, Patrasche! — if I could only see them!"

What were they? pondered Patrasche, looking up with large, wistful, sympathetic eyes.

One day, when the custodian was out of the way and the doors left ajar, he got in for a moment after his little friend and saw. "They" were two great covered pictures on either side of the choir.

Nello was kneeling, rapt as in an ecstasy, before the altar-picture of the Assumption, and when he noticed Patrasche, and rose and drew the dog gently out into the air, his face was wet with tears, and he looked up at the veiled places as he passed them, and murmured to his companion, "It is so terrible not to see them, Patrasche, just because one is poor and cannot pay! He never meant that the poor should not see them when he painted them, I am sure. He would have had us see them any day, every day: that I am sure. And they keep them shrouded there — shrouded in the dark, the beautiful things! — and they never feel the light, and no eyes look on them, unless rich people come and pay. If I could only see them, I would be content to die."

But he could not see them, and Patrasche could not help him, for to gain the silver piece that the church exacts as the price for looking on the glories of the Elevation of the Cross and the Descent of the Cross was a thing as utterly beyond the powers of either of them as it would have been to scale the heights of the cathedral spire. They had never so much as a sou to spare: if they cleared enough to get a little wood for the stove, a little broth for the pot, it was the utmost they could do. And yet the heart of the child was set in sore and endless longing upon beholding the greatness of the two veiled Rubens.

The whole soul of the little Ardennois thrilled and stirred with an absorbing passion for Art. Going on his ways through the old city in the early days before the sun or the people had risen, Nello, who looked only a little peasant-boy, with a great dog drawing milk to sell from door to door, was in a heaven of dreams whereof Rubens was the god. Nello, cold and hungry, with stockingless feet in wooden shoes, and the winter winds blowing among his curls and lifting his poor thin garments, was in a rapture of meditation, wherein all that he saw was the beautiful fair face of the Mary of the Assumption, with the waves of her golden hair lying upon her shoulders, and the light of an eternal sun shining down upon her brow. Nello, reared in poverty, and buffeted by fortune, and untaught in letters, and unheeded by men, had the compensation or the curse which is called Genius.

No one knew it. He as little as any. No one knew it. Only indeed Patrasche, who, being with him always, saw him draw with chalk upon the stones any and every thing that grew or breathed, heard him on his littlebed of hay murmur all manner of timid, pathetic prayers to the spirit of the great Master; watched his gaze darken and his face radiate at the evening glow of sunset or the rosy rising of the dawn; and felt many and many a time the tears of a strange, nameless pain and joy, mingled together, fall hotly from the bright young eyes upon his own wrinkled yellow forehead.

"I should go to my grave quite content if I thought, Nello, that when thou growest a man thou couldst own this hut and the little plot of ground, and labor for thyself, and be called Baas by thy neighbors," said the old man Jehan many an hour from his bed. For to own a bit of soil, and to be called Baas — master — by the hamlet round, is to have achieved the highest ideal of a Flemish peasant; and the old soldier, who had wandered over all the earth in his youth, and had brought nothing back, deemed in his old age that to live and die on one spot in contented humility was the fairest fate he could desire for his darling. But Nello said nothing.

The same leaven was working in him that in other times begat Rubens and Jordaens and the Van Eycks, and all their wondrous tribe, and in times more recent begat in the green country of the Ardennes, where the Meuse washes the old walls of Dijon, the great artist of the Patroclus, whose genius is too near us for us aright to measure its divinity.

Nello dreamed of other things in the future than of tilling the little rood of earth, and living under the wattle roof, and being called Baas by neighbors a little poorer or a little less poor than himself. The cathedral spire, where it rose beyond the fields in the ruddy evening skies or in the dim, gray, misty mornings, said other things to him than this. But these he told only to Patrasche, whispering, childlike, his fancies in the dog's ear when they went together at their work through the fogs of the daybreak, or lay together at their rest among the rustling rushes by the water's side.

For such dreams are not easily shaped into speech to awake the slow sympathies of human auditors; and they would only have sorely perplexed and troubled the poor old man bedridden in his corner, who, for his part, whenever he had trodden the streets of Antwerp, had thought the daub of blue and red that they called a Madonna, on the walls of the wine-shop where he drank his sou's worth of black beer, quite as good as any of the famous altar-pieces for which the stranger folk travelled far and wide into Flanders from every land on which the good sun shone.

 4

There was only one other beside Patrasche to whom Nello could talk at all of his daring fantasies. This other was little Alois, who lived at the old red mill on the grassy mound, and whose father, the miller, was the best-to-do husbandman in all the village. Little Alois was only a pretty baby with soft round, rosy features, made lovely by those sweet dark eyes that the Spanish rule has left in so many a Flemish face, in testimony of the Alvan dominion, as Spanish art has left broadsown throughout the country majestic palaces and stately courts, gilded house-fronts and sculptured lintels — histories in blazonry and poems in stone.

Little Alois was often with Nello and Patrasche. They played in the fields, they ran in the snow, they gathered the daisies and bilberries, they went up to the old gray church together, and they often sat together by the broad wood-fire in the mill-house. Little Alois, indeed, was the richest child in the hamlet. She had neither brother nor sister; her blue serge dress had never a hole in it; at Kermesse she had as many gilded nuts and Agni Dei in sugar as her hands could hold; and when she went up for her first communion her flaxen curls were covered with a cap of richest Mechlin lace, which had been her mother's and her grandmother's before it came to her. Men spoke already, though she had but twelve years, of the good wife she would be for their sons to woo and win; but she herself was a little gay, simple child, in nowise conscious of her heritage, and she loved no playfellows so well as Jehan Daas's grandson and his dog.

One day her father, Baas Cogez, a good man, but somewhat stern, came on a pretty group in the long meadow behind the mill, where the aftermath had that day been cut. It was his little daughter sitting amidst the hay, with the great tawny head of Patrasche on her lap, and many wreaths of poppies and blue corn-flowers round them both: on a clean smooth slab of pine wood the boy Nello drew their likeness with a stick of charcoal.

The miller stood and looked at the portrait with tears in his eyes, it was so strangely like, and he loved his only child closely and well. Then he roughly chid the little girl for idling there whilst her mother needed her within, and sent her indoors crying and afraid: then, turning, he snatched the wood from Nello's hands. "Dost do much of such folly?" he asked, but there was a tremble in his voice.

Nello colored and hung his head. "I draw everything I see," he murmured.

The miller was silent: then he stretched his hand out with a franc in it. "It is folly, as I say, and evil waste of time: nevertheless, it is like Alois, and will please the house-mother. Take this silver bit for it and leave it for me."

The color died out of the face of the young Ardennois; he lifted his head and put his hands behind his back. "Keep your money and the portrait both, Baas Cogez," he said, simply. "You have been often good to me." Then he called Patrasche to him, and walked away across the field.

"I could have seen them with that franc," he murmured to Patrasche, "but I could not sell her picture — not even for them."

Baas Cogez went into his mill-house sore troubled in his mind.

"That lad must not be so much with Alois," he said to his wife that night. "Trouble may come of it hereafter: he is fifteen now, and she is twelve; and the boy is comely of face and form."

"And he is a good lad and a loyal," said the housewife, feasting her eyes on the piece of pine wood where it was throned above the chimney with a cuckoo clock in oak and a Calvary in wax.

"Yea, I do not gainsay that," said the miller, draining his pewter flagon.

"Then, if what you think of were ever to come to pass," said the wife, hesitatingly, "would it matter so much? She will have enough for both, and one cannot be better than happy."

"You are a woman, and therefore a fool," said the miller, harshly, striking his pipe on the table. "The lad is naught but a beggar, and, with these painter's fancies, worse than a beggar. Have a care that they are not together in the future, or I will send the child to the surer keeping of the nuns of the Sacred Heart."

The poor mother was terrified, and promised humbly to do his will. Not that she could bring herself altogether to separate the child from her favorite playmate, nor did the miller even desire that extreme of cruelty to a young lad who was guilty of nothing except poverty. But there were many ways in which little Alois was kept away from her chosen companion; and Nello, being a boy proud and quiet and sensitive, was quickly wounded, and ceased to turn his own steps and those of Patrasche, as he had been used to do with every moment of leisure, to the old red mill upon the slope. What his offence was he did not know: he supposed he had in some manner angered Baas Cogez by taking the portrait of Alois in the meadow; and when the child who loved him would run to him and nestle her hand in his, he would smile at her very sadly and say with a tender concern for her before himself, "Nay, Alois, do not anger your father. He thinks that I make you idle, dear, and he is not pleased that you should be with me. He is a good man and loves you well: we will not anger him, Alois."

But it was with a sad heart that he said it, and the earth did not look so bright to him as it had used to do when he went out at sunrise under the poplars down the straight roads with Patrasche. The old red mill had been a landmark to him, and he had been used to pause by it, going and coming, for a cheery greeting with its people as her little flaxen head rose above the low mill-wicket, and her little rosy hands had held out a bone or a crust to Patrasche. Now the dog looked wistfully at a closed door, and the boy went on without pausing, with a pang at his heart, and the child sat within with tears dropping slowly on the knitting to which she was set on her little stool by the stove; and Baas Cogez, working among his sacks and his mill-gear, would harden his will and say to himself, "It is best so. The lad is all but a beggar, and full of idle, dreaming fooleries. Who knows what mischief might not come of it in the future?"

So he was wise in his generation, and would not have the door unbarred, except upon rare and formal occasion, which seemed to have neither warmth nor mirth in them to the two children, who had been accustomed so long to a daily gleeful, careless, happy interchange of greeting, speech, and pastime, with no other watcher of their sports or auditor of their fancies than Patrasche, sagely shaking the brazen bells of his collar and responding with all a dog's swift sympathies to their every change of mood.

All this while the little panel of pine wood remained over the chimney in the mill-kitchen with the cuckoo clock and the waxen

Calvary, and sometimes it seemed to Nello a little hard that whilst his gift was accepted he himself should be denied.

But he did not complain: it was his habit to be quiet: old Jehan Daas had said ever to him, "We are poor: we must take what God sends — the ill with the good: the poor cannot choose."

To which the boy had always listened in silence, being reverent of his old grandfather; but nevertheless a certain vague, sweet hope, such as beguiles the children of genius, had whispered in his heart, "Yet the poor do choose sometimes — choose to be great, so that men cannot say them nay." And he thought so still in his innocence; and one day, when the little Alois, finding him by chance alone among the cornfields by the canal, ran to him and held him close, and sobbed piteously because the morrow would be her saint's day, and for the first time in all her life her parents had failed to bid him to the little supper and romp in the great barns with which her feast-day was always celebrated, Nello had kissed her and murmured to her in firm faith, "It shall be different one day, Alois. One day that little bit of pine wood that your father has of mine shall be worth its weight in silver; and he will not shut the door against me then. Only love me always, dear little Alois, only love me always, and I will be great."

"And if I do not love you?" the pretty child asked, pouting a little through her tears, and moved by the instinctive coquetries of her sex.

Nello's eyes left her face and wandered to the distance, where in the red and gold of the Flemish night the cathedral spire rose. There was a smile on his face so sweet and yet so sad that little Alois was awed by it. "I will be great still," he said under his breath —" great still, or die, Alois."

"You do not love me," said the little spoilt child, pushing him away; but the boy shook his head and smiled, and went on his way through the tall yellow corn, seeing as in a vision some day in a fair future when he should come into that old familiar land and ask Alois of her people, and be not refused or denied, but received in honor, whilst the village folk should throng to look upon him and say in one another's ears, "Dost see him? He is a king among men, for he is a great artist and the world speaks his name; and yet he was only our poor little Nello, who was a beggar as one may say, and only got his bread by the help of his dog." And he thought how he would fold his grandsire in furs and purples, and portray him as the old man is portrayed in the Family in the chapel of St. Jacques; and of how he would hang the throat of Patrasche with a collar of gold, and place him on his right hand, and say to the people, "This was once my only friend;" and of how he would build himself a great white marble palace, and make to himself luxuriant gardens of pleasure, on the slope looking outward to where the cathedral spire rose, and not dwell in it himself, but summon to it, as to a home, all men young and poor and friendless, but of the will to do mighty things; and of how he would say to them always, if they sought to bless his name, "Nay, do not thank me — thank Rubens. Without him, what should I have been?" And these dreams, beautiful, impossible, innocent, free of all selfishness, full of heroical worship, were so closely about him as he went that he was happy — happy even on this sad anniversary of Alois's saint's day, when he and Patrasche went home by themselves to the little dark hut and the meal of black bread, whilst in the mill-house all the children of the village sang and laughed, and ate the big round cakes of Dijon and the almond gingerbread of Brabant, and danced in the great barn to the light of the stars and the music of flute and fiddle.

"Never mind, Patrasche," he said, with his arms round the dog's neck as they both sat in the door of the hut, where the sounds of the mirth at the mill came down to them on the night air —" never mind. It shall all be changed by and by."

He believed in the future: Patrasche, of more experience and of more philosophy, thought that the loss of the mill supper in the present was ill compensated by dreams of milk and honey in some vague hereafter. And Patrasche growled whenever he passed by Baas Cogez.

"This is Alois's name-day, is it not?" said the old man Daas that night from the corner where he was stretched upon his bed of sacking.

The boy gave a gesture of assent: he wished that the old man's memory had erred a little, instead of keeping such sure account.

"And why not there?" his grandfather pursued. "Thou hast never missed a year before, Nello."

"Thou art too sick to leave," murmured the lad, bending his handsome head over the bed.

"Tut! Tut! Mother Nulette would have come and sat with me, as she does scores of times. What is the cause, Nello?" the old man persisted. "Thou surely hast not had ill words with the little one?"

"Nay, grandfather — never," said the boy quickly, with a hot color in his bent face. "Simply and truly, Baas Cogez did not have me asked this year. He has taken some whim against me."

"But thou hast done nothing wrong?"

"That I know — nothing. I took the portrait of Alois on a piece of pine: that is all."

"Ah!" The old man was silent: the truth suggested itself to him with the boy's innocent answer. He was tied to a bed of dried leaves in the corner of a wattle hut, but he had not wholly forgotten what the ways of the world were like.

He drew Nello's fair head fondly to his breast with a tenderer gesture. "Thou art very poor, my child," he said with a quiver the more in his aged, trembling voice —" so poor! It is very hard for thee."

"Nay, I am rich," murmured Nello; and in his innocence he thought so — rich with the imperishable powers that are mightier than the might of kings.

And he went and stood by the door of the hut in the quiet autumn night, and watched the stars troop by and the tall poplars bend and shiver in the wind. All the casements of the mill-house were lighted, and every now and then the notes of the flute came to him. The tears fell down his cheeks, for he was but a child, yet he smiled, for he said to himself, "In the future!" He stayed there until all was quite still and dark, then he and Patrasche went within and slept together, long and deeply, side by side.

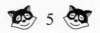

5

Now he had a secret which only Patrasche knew. There was a little out-house to the hut, which no one entered but himself — a dreary place, but with abundant clear light from the north. Here he had fashioned himself rudely an easel in rough lumber, and here on a great gray sea of stretched paper he had given shape to one of the innumerable fancies which possessed his brain. No one had ever

taught him anything; colors he had no means to buy; he had gone
without bread many a time to procure even the few rude vehicles
that he had here; and it was only in black or white that he could
fashion the things he saw. This great figure which he had drawn
here in chalk was only an old man sitting on a fallen tree — only
that.

He had seen old Michel the woodman sitting so at evening many a
time. He had never had a soul to tell him of outline or perspective,
of anatomy or of shadow, and yet he had given all the weary, worn-
out age, all the sad, quiet patience, all the rugged, careworn pathos
of his original, and given them so that the old lonely figure was a
poem, sitting there, meditative and alone, on the dead tree, with the
darkness of the descending night behind him.

It was rude, of course, in a way, and had many faults, no doubt; and
yet it was real, true in nature, true in art, and very mournful, and in
a manner beautiful.

Patrasche had lain quiet countless hours watching its gradual
creation after the labor of each day was done, and he knew that
Nello had a hope — vain and wild perhaps, but strongly cherished
— of sending this great drawing to compete for a prize of two
hundred francs a year which it was announced in Antwerp would be
open to every lad of talent, scholar or peasant, under eighteen, who
would attempt to win it with some unaided work of chalk or pencil.
Three of the foremost artists in the town of Rubens were to be the
judges and elect the victor according to his merits.

All the spring and summer and autumn Nello had been at work
upon this treasure, which, if triumphant, would build him his first
step toward independence and the mysteries of the art which he
blindly, ignorantly, and yet passionately adored.

He said nothing to any one: his grandfather would not have understood, and little Alois was lost to him. Only to Patrasche he told all, and whispered, "Rubens would give it me, I think, if he knew."

Patrasche thought so too, for he knew that Rubens had loved dogs or he had never painted them with such exquisite fidelity; and men who loved dogs were, as Patrasche knew, always pitiful.

The drawings were to go in on the first day of December, and the decision be given on the twenty-fourth, so that he who should win might rejoice with all his people at the Christmas season.

In the twilight of a bitter wintry day, and with a beating heart, now quick with hope, now faint with fear, Nello placed the great picture on his little green milk-cart, and took it, with the help of Patrasche, into the town, and there left it, as enjoined, at the doors of a public building.

"Perhaps it is worth nothing at all. How can I tell?" he thought, with the heart-sickness of a great timidity. Now that he had left it there, it seemed to him so hazardous, so vain, so foolish, to dream that he, a little lad with bare feet, who barely knew his letters, could do anything at which great painters, real artists, could ever deign to look. Yet he took heart as he went by the cathedral: the lordly form of Rubens seemed to rise from the fog and the darkness, and to loom in its magnificence before him, whilst the lips, with their kindly smile, seemed to him to murmur, "Nay, have courage! It was not by a weak heart and by faint fears that I wrote my name for all time upon Antwerp."

Nello ran home through the cold night, comforted. He had done his best: the rest must be as God willed, he thought, in that innocent, unquestioning faith which had been taught him in the little gray chapel among the willows and the poplar-trees.

The winter was very sharp already. That night, after they reached the hut, snow fell; and fell for very many days after that, so that the paths and the divisions in the fields were all obliterated, and all the smaller streams were frozen over, and the cold was intense upon the plains. Then, indeed, it became hard work to go round for the milk while the world was all dark, and carry it through the darkness to the silent town. Hard work, especially for Patrasche, for the passage of the years, that were only bringing Nello a stronger youth, were bringing him old age, and his joints were stiff and his bones ached often. But he would never give up his share of the labor. Nello would fain have spared him and drawn the cart himself, but Patrasche would not allow it. All he would ever permit or accept was the help of a thrust from behind to the truck as it lumbered along through the ice-ruts. Patrasche had lived in harness, and he was proud of it. He suffered a great deal sometimes from frost, and the terrible roads, and the rheumatic pains of his limbs, but he only drew his breath hard and bent his stout neck, and trod onward with steady patience.

"Rest thee at home, Patrasche — it is time thou didst rest — and I can quite well push in the cart by myself," urged Nello many a morning; but Patrasche, who understood him aright, would no more have consented to stay at home than a veteran soldier to shirk when the charge was sounding; and every day he would rise and place himself in his shafts, and plod along over the snow through the fields that his four round feet had left their print upon so many, many years.

"One must never rest till one dies," thought Patrasche; and sometimes it seemed to him that that time of rest for him was not very far off. His sight was less clear than it had been, and it gave him pain to rise after the night's sleep, though he would never lie a moment in his straw when once the bell of the chapel tolling five let him know that the daybreak of labor had begun.

"My poor Patrasche, we shall soon lie quiet together, you and I," said old Jehan Daas, stretching out to stroke the head of Patrasche with the old withered hand which had always shared with him its one poor crust of bread; and the hearts of the old man and the old dog ached together with one thought: When they were gone, who would care for their darling?

One afternoon, as they came back from Antwerp over the snow, which had become hard and smooth as marble over all the Flemish plains, they found dropped in the road a pretty little puppet, a tambourine — player, all scarlet and gold, about six inches high, and, unlike greater personages when Fortune lets them drop, quite unspoiled and unhurt by its fall. It was a pretty toy. Nello tried to find its owner, and, failing, thought that it was just the thing to please Alois.

It was quite night when he passed the mill-house: he knew the little window of her room. It could be no harm, he thought, if he gave her his little piece of treasure-trove, they had been playfellows so long. There was a shed with a sloping roof beneath her casement: he climbed it and tapped softly at the lattice: there was a little light within. The child opened it and looked out half frightened. Nello put the tambourine-player into her hands. "Here is a doll I found in the snow, Alois. Take it," he whispered —" take it, and God bless thee, dear!"

He slid down from the shed-roof before she had time to thank him, and ran off through the darkness.

6

That night there was a fire at the mill. Outbuildings and much corn were destroyed, although the mill itself and the dwelling-house were unharmed.

All the village was out in terror, and engines came tearing through the snow from Antwerp. The miller was insured, and would lose nothing: nevertheless, he was in furious wrath, and declared aloud that the fire was due to no accident, but to some foul intent.

Nello, awakened from his sleep, ran to help with the rest: Baas Cogez thrust him angrily aside. "Thou wert loitering here after dark," he said roughly. "I believe, on my soul, that thou dost know more of the fire than any one."

Nello heard him in silence, stupefied, not supposing that anyone could say such things except in jest, and not comprehending how anyone could pass a jest at such a time.

Nevertheless, the miller said the brutal thing openly to many of his neighbors in the day that followed; and though no serious charge was ever preferred against the lad, it got bruited about that Nello had been seen in the mill-yard after dark on some unspoken errand, and that he bore Baas Cogez a grudge for forbidding his intercourse with little Alois; and so the hamlet, which followed the sayings of its richest landowner servilely, and whose families all hoped to secure the riches of Alois in some future time for their sons, took the hint to give grave looks and cold words to old Jehan Daas's grandson. No one said anything to him openly, but all the village agreed together to humor the miller's prejudice, and at the cottages and farms where Nello and Patrasche called every morning for the milk for Antwerp, downcast glances and brief phrases replaced

to them the broad smiles and cheerful greetings to which they
had been always used. No one really credited the miller's absurd
suspicion, nor the outrageous accusations born of them, but the
people were all very poor and very ignorant, and the one rich man
of the place had pronounced against him.

Nello, in his innocence and his friendlessness, had no strength to
stem the popular tide.

"Thou art very cruel to the lad," the miller's wife dared to say,
weeping, to her lord. "Sure he is an innocent lad and a faithful, and
would never dream of any such wickedness, however sore his heart
might be."

But Baas Cogez being an obstinate man, having once said a thing
held to it doggedly, though in his innermost soul he knew well the
injustice that he was committing.

Meanwhile, Nello endured the injury done against him with a
certain proud patience that disdained to complain: he only gave
way a little when he was quite alone with old Patrasche. Besides, he
thought, "If it should win! They will be sorry then, perhaps."

Still, to a boy not quite sixteen, and who had dwelt in one little
world all his short life, and in his childhood had been caressed
and applauded on all sides, it was a hard trial to have the whole
of that little world turn against him for naught. Especially hard
in that bleak, snow-bound, famine-stricken winter-time, when
the only light and warmth there could be found abode beside the
village hearths and in the kindly greetings of neighbors. In the
winter-time all drew nearer to each other, all to all, except to Nello
and Patrasche, with whom none now would have anything to do,
and who were left to fare as they might with the old paralyzed,
bedridden man in the little cabin, whose fire was often low, and

whose board was often without bread, for there was a buyer from Antwerp who had taken to drive his mule in of a day for the milk of the various dairies, and there were only three or four of the people who had refused his terms of purchase and remained faithful to the little green cart. So that the burden which Patrasche drew had become very light, and the centime-pieces in Nello's pouch had become, alas! Very small likewise.

The dog would stop, as usual, at all the familiar gates, which were now closed to him, and look up at them with wistful, mute appeal; and it cost the neighbors a pang to shut their doors and their hearts, and let Patrasche draw his cart on again, empty. Nevertheless, they did it, for they desired to please Baas Cogez.

Noël was close at hand.

The weather was very wild and cold. The snow was six feet deep, and the ice was firm enough to bear oxen and men upon it everywhere. At this season the little village was always gay and cheerful. At the poorest dwelling there were possets and cakes, joking and dancing, sugared saints and gilded Jésus. The merry Flemish bells jingled everywhere on the horses; everywhere within doors some well-filled soup-pot sang and smoked over the stove; and everywhere over the snow without laughing maidens pattered in bright kerchiefs and stout kirtles, going to and from the mass. Only in the little hut it was very dark and very cold.

Nello and Patrasche were left utterly alone, for one night in the week before the Christmas Day, Death entered there, and took away from life forever old Jehan Daas, who had never known life aught save its poverty and its pains. He had long been half dead, incapable of any movement except a feeble gesture, and powerless for anything beyond a gentle word; and yet his loss fell on them both with a great horror in it: they mourned him passionately. He had passed away from them in his sleep, and when in the gray dawn they learned their bereavement, unutterable solitude and desolation seemed to close around them. He had long been only a poor, feeble, paralyzed old man, who could not raise a hand in their defence, but he had loved them well: his smile had always welcomed their return. They mourned for him unceasingly, refusing to be comforted, as in the white winter day they followed the deal shell that held his body to the nameless grave by the little gray church. They were his only mourners, these two whom he had left friendless upon earth — the young boy and the old dog.

"Surely, he will relent now and let the poor lad come hither?" thought the miller's wife, glancing at her husband smoking by the hearth.

Baas Cogez knew her thought, but he hardened his heart, and would not unbar his door as the little, humble funeral went by. "The boy is a beggar," he said to himself: "he shall not be about Alois."

The woman dared not say anything aloud, but when the grave was closed and the mourners had gone, she put a wreath of immortelles into Alois's hands and bade her go and lay it reverently on the dark, unmarked mound where the snow was displaced.

 7

Nello and Patrasche went home with broken hearts. But even of that poor, melancholy, cheerless home they were denied the consolation. There was a month's rent over-due for their little home, and when

Nello had paid the last sad service to the dead he had not a coin left. He went and begged grace of the owner of the hut, a cobbler who went every Sunday night to drink his pint of wine and smoke with Baas Cogez. The cobbler would grant no mercy. He was a harsh, miserly man, and loved money. He claimed in default of his rent every stick and stone, every pot and pan, in the hut, and bade Nello and Patrasche be out of it on the morrow.

Now, the cabin was lowly enough, and in some sense miserable enough, and yet their hearts clove to it with a great affection. They had been so happy there, and in the summer, with its clambering vine and its flowering beans, it was so pretty and bright in the midst of the sunlighted fields!

There life in it had been full of labor and privation, and yet they had been so well content, so gay of heart, running together to meet the old man's never-failing smile of welcome!

All night long the boy and the dog sat by the fireless hearth in the darkness, drawn close together for warmth and sorrow. Their bodies were insensible to the cold, but their hearts seemed frozen in them. When the morning broke over the white, chill earth it was the morning of Christmas Eve. With a shudder, Nello clasped close to him his only friend, while his tears fell hot and fast on the dog's frank forehead. "Let us go, Patrasche — dear, dear Patrasche," he murmured. "We will not wait to be kicked out: let us go."

Patrasche had no will but his, and they went sadly, side by side, out from the little place which was so dear to them both, and in which every humble, homely thing was to them precious and beloved. Patrasche drooped his head wearily as he passed by his own green cart: it was no longer his — it had to go with the rest to pay the rent, and his brass harness lay idle and glittering on the snow. The dog could have lain down beside it and died for very heart-sickness as he went, but whilst the lad lived and needed him Patrasche would not yield and give way.

They took the old accustomed road into Antwerp. The day had yet scarce more than dawned, most of the shutters were still closed, but some of the villagers were about. They took no notice whilst the dog and the boy passed by them. At one door Nello paused and looked wistfully within: his grandfather had done many a kindly turn in neighbor's service to the people who dwelt there.

"Would you give Patrasche a crust?" he said, timidly. "He is old, and he has had nothing since last forenoon."

The woman shut the door hastily, murmuring some vague saying about wheat and rye being very dear that season. The boy and the dog went on again wearily: they asked no more.

By slow and painful ways they reached Antwerp as the chimes tolled ten.

"If I had anything about me I could sell to get him bread!" thought Nello, but he had nothing except the wisp of linen and serge that covered him, and his pair of wooden shoes. Patrasche understood, and nestled his nose into the lad's hand, as though to pray him not to be disquieted for any woe or want of his.

The winner of the drawing-prize was to be proclaimed at noon, and to the public building where he had left his treasure Nello made his way. On the steps and in the entrance-hall there was a crowd of youths — some of his age, some older, all with parents or relatives or friends. His heart was sick with fear as he went among them, holding Patrasche close to him. The great bells of the city clashed out the hour of noon with brazen clamor.

The doors of the inner hall were opened; the eager, panting throng rushed in: it was known that the selected picture would be raised above the rest upon a wooden dais.

A mist obscured Nello's sight, his head swam, his limbs almost failed him.

When his vision cleared he saw the drawing raised on high: it was not his own! A slow, sonorous voice was proclaiming aloud that victory had been adjudged to Stephen Kiesslinger, born in the burgh of Antwerp, son of a wharfinger in that town.

When Nello recovered his consciousness he was lying on the stones without, and Patrasche was trying with every art he knew to call him back to life.

In the distance a throng of the youths of Antwerp were shouting around their successful comrade, and escorting him with acclamations to his home upon the quay.

The boy staggered to his feet and drew the dog into his embrace. "It is all over, dear Patrasche," he murmured —" all over!"

He rallied himself as best he could, for he was weak from fasting, and retraced his steps to the village. Patrasche paced by his side with his head drooping and his old limbs feeble from hunger and sorrow.

The snow was falling fast: a keen hurricane blew from the north: it was bitter as death on the plains. It took them long to traverse the familiar path, and the bells were sounding four of the clock as they approached the hamlet. Suddenly Patrasche paused, arrested by a scent in the snow, scratched, whined, and drew out with his teeth a small case of brown leather. He held it up to Nello in the darkness. Where they were there stood a little Calvary, and a lamp burned dully under the cross: the boy mechanically turned the case to the light: on it was the name of Baas Cogez, and within it were notes for two thousand francs.

The sight roused the lad a little from his stupor. He thrust it in his shirt, and stroked Patrasche and drew him onward. The dog looked up wistfully in his face.

Nello made straight for the mill-house, and went to the house-door and struck on its panels. The miller's wife opened it weeping, with little Alois clinging close to her skirts. "Is it thee, thou poor lad?" she said kindly through her tears. "Get thee gone ere the Baas see thee. We are in sore trouble to-night. He is out seeking for a power of money that he has let fall riding homeward, and in this snow he never will find it; and God knows it will go nigh to ruin us. It is Heaven's own judgment for the things we have done to thee."

Nello put the note-case in her hand and called Patrasche within the house.

"Patrasche found the money to-night," he said quickly. "Tell Baas Cogez so: I think he will not deny the dog shelter and food in his old age. Keep him from pursuing me, and I pray of you to be good to him."

Ere either woman or dog knew what he meant he had stooped and kissed Patrasche: then closed the door hurriedly, and disappeared in the gloom of the fast — falling night.

The woman and the child stood speechless with joy and fear: Patrasche vainly spent the fury of his anguish against the iron-bound oak of the barred house-door. They did not dare unbar the door and let him forth: they tried all they could to solace him. They brought him sweet cakes and juicy meats; they tempted him with the best they had; they tried to lure him to abide by the warmth of the hearth; but it was of no avail.

Patrasche refused to be comforted or to stir from the barred portal.

It was six o'clock when from an opposite entrance the miller at last came, jaded and broken, into his wife's presence. "It is lost forever," he said, with an ashen cheek and a quiver in his stern voice. "We have looked with lanterns everywhere: it is gone — the little maiden's portion and all!"

His wife put the money into his hand, and told him how it had come to her.

The strong man sank trembling into a seat and covered his face, ashamed and almost afraid. "I have been cruel to the lad," he muttered at length: "I deserved not to have good at his hands." Little Alois, taking courage, crept close to her father and nestled against him her fair curly head. "Nello may come here again, father?" she whispered. "He may come to-morrow as he used to do?"

The miller pressed her in his arms: his hard, sunburned face was very pale and his mouth trembled. "Surely, surely," he answered his child. "He shall bide here on Christmas Day, and any other day he will. God helping me, I will make amends to the boy — I will make amends."

Little Alois kissed him in gratitude and joy, then slid from his knees and ran to where the dog kept watch by the door. "And to-night I may feast Patrasche?" she cried in a child's thoughtless glee.

Her father bent his head gravely: "Ay, ay: let the dog have the best;" for the stern old man was moved and shaken to his heart's depths.

It was Christmas Eve, and the mill-house was filled with oak logs and squares of turf, with cream and honey, with meat and bread, and the rafters were hung with wreaths of evergreen, and the Calvary and the cuckoo clock looked out from a mass of holly. There were little paper lanterns, too, for Alois, and toys of various fashions and sweetmeats in bright-pictured papers. There were light and warmth and abundance everywhere, and the child would fain have made the dog a guest honored and feasted.

But Patrasche would neither lie in the warmth nor share in the cheer. Famished he was and very cold, but without Nello he would partake neither of comfort nor food. Against all temptation he was proof, and close against the door he leaned always, watching only for a means of escape.

"He wants the lad," said Baas Cogez. "Good dog! Good dog! I will go over to the lad the first thing at day-dawn." For no one but Patrasche knew that Nello had left the hut, and no one but Patrasche divined that Nello had gone to face starvation and misery alone. The mill-kitchen was very warm: great logs crackled and flamed on the hearth; neighbors came in for a glass of wine and a slice of the fat goose baking for supper. Alois, gleeful and sure of her playmate back on the morrow, bounded and sang and tossed back her yellow hair. Baas Cogez, in the fulness of his heart, smiled on her through moistened eyes, and spoke of the way in which he would befriend her favorite companion; the house-mother sat with calm, contented face at the spinning-wheel; the cuckoo in the clock chirped mirthful hours. Amidst it all Patrasche was bidden with a thousand words of welcome to tarry there a cherished guest.

But neither peace nor plenty could allure him where Nello was not. When the supper smoked on the board, and the voices were loudest and gladdest, and the Christ-child brought choicest gifts to Alois, Patrasche, watching always an occasion, glided out when the door was unlatched by a careless new-comer, and as swiftly as his weak and tired limbs would bear him sped over the snow in the bitter, black night. He had only one thought — to follow Nello. A human friend might have paused for the pleasant meal, the cheery warmth, the cosey slumber; but that was not the friendship of Patrasche. He remembered a bygone time, when an old man and a little child had found him sick unto death in the wayside ditch.

 8

Snow had fallen freshly all the evening long; it was now nearly ten; the trail of the boy's footsteps was almost obliterated. It took Patrasche long to discover any scent. When at last he found it, it was lost again quickly, and lost and recovered, and again lost and again recovered, a hundred times or more.

The night was very wild. The lamps under the wayside crosses were blown out; the roads were sheets of ice; the impenetrable darkness hid every trace of habitations; there was no living thing abroad. All the cattle were housed, and in all the huts and homesteads men and women rejoiced and feasted. There was only Patrasche out in the cruel cold — old and famished and full of pain, but with the strength and the patience of a great love to sustain him in his search. The trail of Nello's steps, faint and obscure as it was under the new snow, went straightly along the accustomed tracks into Antwerp. It was past midnight when Patrasche traced it over the boundaries of the town and into the narrow, tortuous, gloomy streets. It was all quite dark in the town, save where some light gleamed ruddily through the crevices of house-shutters, or some group went homeward with lanterns chanting drinking-songs. The streets were all white with ice: the high walls and roofs loomed black against them. There was scarce a sound save the riot of the winds down the passages as they tossed the creaking signs and shook the tall lamp-irons.

So many passers-by had trodden through and through the snow, so many diverse paths had crossed and recrossed each other, that the dog had a hard task to retain any hold on the track he followed. But he kept on his way, though the cold pierced him to the bone, and the jagged ice cut his feet, and the hunger in his body gnawed like a rat's teeth. He kept on his way, a poor gaunt, shivering thing, and by long patience traced the steps he loved into the very heart of the burgh and up to the steps of the great cathedral.

"He is gone to the things that he loved," thought Patrasche: he could not understand, but he was full of sorrow and of pity for the art-passion that to him was so incomprehensible and yet so sacred.

The portals of the cathedral were unclosed after the midnight mass. Some heedlessness in the custodians, too eager to go home and feast or sleep, or too drowsy to know whether they turned the keys aright, had left one of the doors unlocked. By that accident the foot-falls Patrasche sought had passed through into the building, leaving the white marks of snow upon the dark stone floor. By that slender white thread, frozen as it fell, he was guided through the intense silence, through the immensity of the vaulted space — guided straight to the gates of the chancel, and, stretched there upon the stones, he found Nello. He crept up and touched the face of the boy.

"Didst thou dream that I should be faithless and forsake thee? I — a dog?" said that mute caress.

The lad raised himself with a low cry and clasped him close. "Let us lie down and die together," he murmured. "Men have no need of us, and we are all alone."

In answer, Patrasche crept closer yet, and laid his head upon the young boy's breast. The great tears stood in his brown, sad eyes: not for himself — for himself he was happy.

They lay close together in the piercing cold. The blasts that blew over the Flemish dikes from the northern seas were like waves of ice, which froze every living thing they touched. The interior of the immense vault of stone in which they were was even more bitterly chill than the snow-covered plains without. Now and then a bat moved in the shadows — now and then a gleam of light came on the ranks of carven figures. Under the Rubens they lay together quite still, and soothed almost into a dreaming slumber by the numbing narcotic of the cold. Together they dreamed of the old glad days when they had chased each other through the flowering grasses of the summer meadows, or sat hidden in the tall bulrushes by the water's side, watching the boats go seaward in the sun.

Suddenly through the darkness a great white radiance streamed through the vastness of the aisles; the moon, that was at her height, had broken through the clouds, the snow had ceased to fall, the light reflected from the snow without was clear as the light of dawn. It fell through the arches full upon the two pictures above, from which the boy on his entrance had flung back the veil: the Elevation and the Descent of the Cross were for one instant visible.

Nello rose to his feet and stretched his arms to them; the tears of a passionate ecstasy glistened on the paleness of his face. "I have seen them at last!" he cried aloud. "O God, it is enough!"

His limbs failed under him, and he sank upon his knees, still gazing upward at the majesty that he adored. For a few brief moments the light illumined the divine visions that had been denied to him so long — light clear and sweet and strong as though it streamed from the throne of Heaven. Then suddenly it passed away: once more a great darkness covered the face of Christ.

The arms of the boy drew close again the body of the dog. "We shall see His face — there," he murmured; "and He will not part us, I think." On the morrow, by the chancel of the cathedral, the people of Antwerp found them both. They were both dead: the cold of the night had frozen into stillness alike the young life and the old. When the Christmas morning broke and the priests came to the temple, they saw them lying thus on the stones together. Above the veils were drawn back from the great visions of Rubens, and the fresh rays of the sunrise touched the thorn-crowned head of the Christ.

As the day grew on there came an old, hard-featured man who wept as women weep. "I was cruel to the lad," he muttered, "and now I would have made amends — yea, to the half of my substance — and he should have been to me as a son."

There came also, as the day grew apace, a painter who had fame in the world, and who was liberal of hand and of spirit. "I seek one who should have had the prize yesterday had worth won," he said to the people —" a boy of rare promise and genius. An old wood-cutter on a fallen tree at eventide — that was all his theme. But there was greatness for the future in it. I would fain find him, and take him with me and teach him Art."

And a little child with curling fair hair, sobbing bitterly as she clung to her father's arm, cried aloud, "Oh, Nello, come! We have all ready for thee. The Christ-child's hands are full of gifts, and the old piper will play for us; and the mother says thou shalt stay by the hearth and burn nuts with us all the Noël week long — yes, even to the Feast of the Kings!

And Patrasche will be so happy! Oh, Nello, wake and come!"
But the young pale face, turned upward to the light of the great
Rubens with a smile upon its mouth, answered them all, "It is too
late."

For the sweet, sonorous bells went ringing through the frost, and the
sunlight shone upon the plains of snow, and the populace trooped
gay and glad through the streets, but Nello and Patrasche no more
asked charity at their hands. All they needed now Antwerp gave
unbidden.

Death had been more pitiful to them than longer life would have
been. It had taken the one in the loyalty of love, and the other in the
innocence of faith, from a world which for love has no recompense
and for faith no fulfilment.

All their lives they had been together, and in their deaths they were
not divided: for when they were found the arms of the boy were
folded too closely around the dog to be severed without violence,
and the people of their little village, contrite and ashamed, implored
a special grace for them, and, making them one grave, laid them to
rest there side by side — forever!